T0193366

Other Books by the Author

From the Pew to the Pulpit	Published: 08/29/2007
Isaiah 26:3-4 "Perfect Peace"	Published: 09/16/2010*
Isaiah 26:3-4 "Perfect Peace" The Last Single Digit	Published: 02/15/2012*
Isaiah 26:3-4 "Perfect Peace III" Silver and Gold	Published: 10/29/2012*
Isaiah 26:3-4 "Perfect Peace IV" The Kingdom Number	Published: 04/15/2013*
Isaiah 26:3-4 "Perfect Peace V" 2541	Published: 09/13/2013*
Isaiah 26:3-4 "Perfect Peace VI" Zacchaeus	Published: 02/28/2014
Isaiah 26:3-4 "Perfect Peace VII" Eleven	Published: 10/30/2014*
Isaiah 26:3-4 "Perfect Peace VIII" Prayer	Published: 05/21/2015*
Isaiah 26:3-4 "Perfect Peace IX" Sixteen	Published: 10/24/2015*
Isaiah 26:3-4 "Perfect Peace X" Dreams	Published: 04/12/2016
Isaiah 26:3-4 "Perfect Peace XI" Door	Published: 02/13/2017
Isaiah 26:3-4 "Perfect Peace XII" River	Published: 08/02/2017
Isaiah 26:3-4 "Perfect Peace XIII" 1 Kings 19:1-18	Published: 12/18/2017
Isaiah 26:3-4 "Perfect Peace XIV" G – Men	Published: 05/03/2018*
Isaiah 26:3-4 "Perfect Peace XV" 11:29	Published: 07/26/2018
Isaiah 26:3-4 "Perfect Peace XVI" Shoes	Published: 10/31/2018*
Isaiah 26:3-4 "Perfect Peace XVII" Arrow	Published: 01/25/2019*
Isaiah 26:3-4 "Perfect Peace XVIII" Midnight	Published: 04/26/2019
Isaiah 26:3-4 "Perfect Peace XIX" Eyes	Published: 08/20/2019

PS: On 5/25/2019, I noticed that some of the book published dates vary slightly from AuthorHouse, depending on which bookstore site you visit. They have been modified to reflect AuthorHouse's publication date, indicated by an *.

ISAIAH 26:3-4

"PERFECT PEACE XX"

Judges 4:1 - 16

VANESSA RAYNER

authorHOUSE®

AuthorHouse™
1663 Liberty Drive
Bloomington, IN 47403
www.authorhouse.com
Phone: 1 (800) 839-8640

Published by AuthorHouse 12/18/2019

ISBN: 978-1-7283-3986-3 (sc)
ISBN: 978-1-7283-3985-6 (e)

Library of Congress Control Number: 2019920559

Print information available on the last page.

The Scriptures' quotations are taken from the KJV, NLT, ASV, DARBY, DRA, and WEB.

*The King James Version present on the Bible Gateway matches the 1987
printing. The KJV is public domain in the United States.*

*Holy Bible, New Living Translation copyright© 1996, 2004, 2007 by Tyndale
House Foundation. Used by permission of Tyndale House Publishers Inc., Carol
Stream, Illinois 60188. All rights reserved. New Living, NLT, and the New Living
Translation logo are registered trademarks of Tyndale House Publishers.*

*Douay-Rheims Version present on the Bible Gateway is in the public domain.
It is a translation of the Bible from the Latin Vulgate into English made by
members of the Catholic seminary English College, Douai, France. It is the
foundation on which nearly all English Catholic versions are still based.*

*Darby Translation present on the Bible Gateway is in the public domain. John
Nelson Darby was converted in his twenties. He was an Anglo-Irish Bible teacher,
one of the influential figures among the original Plymouth Brethren.*

*American Standard Version present on the Bible Gateway is in the public domain.
It is a revision of the King James Version and was released in 1901.*

*World English Bible present on the Bible Gateway is a public domain. It is an updated
revision of the American Standard Version of the Holy Bible first published in 1901.*

CONTENTS

A GIFT . . .

*P*_{resented to}

_____

*F*_{rom}

_____

*D*_{ate}

_____

There is one Lawgiver, and Judge,
that is able to destroy and
deliver, James 4:12
Douay-Rheims 1899 American Edition (DRA)

THEME

The message of **Isaiah 26:3 – 4** is "Perfect Peace." This message is the distinct and unifying composition of this book with the subtitle "Judges 4:1 – 16."

<u>A Song of Praise</u>

Thou wilt keep him in perfect peace, whose mind is stayed on thee: because he trusted in thee. Trust ye in the LORD for ever: for in the LORD Jehovah is everlasting strength.

Isaiah 26:3 – 4 KJV

PRAYER

Oh, Father God,
I thank you for another day and another
opportunity to write another book.
Oh, Heavenly Fathe r, you have been
good to me, better than I deserve.
Thank You, LORD.
Hallelujah, Glory be to God!

I thank You for blessing my family.
And I pray that your people and their
families are being bless, also.
I pray that people are prospering daily in their spirit,
soul, and body by reading, Perfect Peace Books.

Oh, Heavenly Father,
I ask in Jesus' name that the Holy Spirit will
help readers to remember Your word.
I pray the word of God will give them
peace, at all times, in all situations.

LORD, I thank you for blessing those
that help Your work go forth.
Your word made it clear that You will
reward those that bless your servant.
It could be through prayer, words of
encouragement, to giving that person
a cup of water.

Father God, I like to lift President D. Trump
up to You, in prayer in his trying times.
I give you all the Glory, Honor, and Praise in Jesus' name.

Amen.

AUTHOR'S NOTES

Author notes generally provide a way to add extra information to one's book that may be awkward and inappropriate to include in the text of the book itself. It offers supplemental contextual details on the aspects of the book. It can help readers understand the book content and the background details of the book better. The times and dates of researching, reading, and gathering this information are not included; mostly when I typed on it.

1847; Monday, 08 July 2019

1810; Monday, 15 July 2019

2037; Tuesday, 16 July 2019; I must put this book on hold for several days. AuthorHouse needs me to make some changes to <u>Isaiah 26:3 – 4 "Perfect Peace XIX" Eyes</u>.

0739; Sunday, 11 August 2019

1624; Monday, 12 August 2019

1846; Tuesday, 13 August 2019

2213; Wednesday, 14 August 2019; Just finished looking over <u>Isaiah 26:3-4 "Perfect Peace XIX" Eyes</u> Book Cover/Gallery Proofs.

1814; Thursday, August 15, 2019; A Lovely Workday, today! Praise God.

0837; Saturday, 17 August 2019

2128; Monday, 19 August 2019

1740; Tuesday, 20 August 2019

2142; Thursday, 22 August 2019

2129; Saturday, 24 August 2019; I just got back from Louisville, Kentucky, a few minutes ago. Prophet

Daniel and I attended the Anointed Women Empowered (AWE) Conference hosted by Apostle Jacqueline Herring at the Hilton Gardens, 9850 Park Place, Louisville, KY 40241. The theme was "Wildflowers." It was Hallelujah Awesome! The 4 guest speakers, along with Apostle J. Herring, are truly anointed; Evangelist C. Whitaker, Evangelist A. Gatin, Prophetess R. Denman, and Apostle T. Sharp!

0722;   Sunday, 25 August 2019; I feel renewed, refreshed, and my spiritual being has been washed, cleanse, and re-dipped in the Blood of Christ. Hallelujah! Praise God! I feel a shifting in the atmosphere. Father God is about to do a new thing in my life. I don't know what, or exactly when, but it will be soon. Shatua Maisha . . . .

1922;   Monday, 26 August 2019

1737;   Wednesday, 28 August 2019

1728;   hursday, 29 August 2019

0636;   Sunday, 01 September 2019

0721;   Monday, 02 September 2019; Labor Day

1936;   Wednesday, 04 September 2019

1754;   Thursday, 05 September 2019

2216;   Friday, 06 September 2019; Happy Birthday Dad ~ Rev. Ambous Lee Moore

0000;   Saturday, 07 September 2019

0541;   Saturday, 14 September 2019; Glory Be To God! I took a week off from writing for my eyes; they feel so much better. Praise, God!

1029;   Sunday, 15 September 2019

1836;   Tuesday, 17 September 2019

1719;   Friday, 20 September 2019

0808; Sunday, 22 September 2019; Early yesterday morning, I drove to the Ark Encounter in Williamstown, Kentucky, a round trip of 924.8 miles by myself. I drove exactly 470.0 miles to get to the Ark Encounter' parking lot. My GPS took me home another way, and I drove only 454.8 miles back. It was worth the drive. I listened to Pastor JoAnn's 6 am Early Morning Prayer Line and Prophet Cary L. Allen's 7 pm Empowerment Prayer Line. Now, in between, I listened to two gospel CDs I created in 1/17/2006 and 8/15/2012, several times. I listened to sermons by Bishop G. E. Patterson (The Choice is Yours); Dr. Charles Stanley (Help is On the Way); Dr. Frank E. Ray (Hands); and Minister Joe Brewer, a co-worker of mine around 2009 (Similac Christians). I feel O, so renewed for my journey with the LORD, Hallelujah! (Wrist Band #34431)

2305; Monday, 23 September 2019

0000; Tuesday, 24 September 2019

1838; Wednesday, 25 September 2019

0150; Sunday, 29 September 2019; I have been having red-eye issues again. Praise God, in the midst of it; He sees and knows all.

1920; Tuesday, 01 October 2019

1910; Thursday, 03 October 2019

0016; Saturday, 05 October 2019

0802; Sunday, 06 October 2019

2230; Wednesday, 09 October 2019

1745; Thursday, 10 October 2019

0646; Saturday, 12 October 2019

0513; Sunday, 13 October 2019

1718; Monday, 14 October 2019

1831;   Tuesday, 15 October 2019
1711;   Wednesday, 16 October 2019
1718;   Thursday, 17 October 2019
1730;   Friday, 18 October 2019
0643;   Saturday, 19 October 2019
0643;   Sunday, 20 October 2019; How unique . . . I'm sitting down at the exact time as yesterday morning, to work on this book. Father God is awesome.
1714;   Monday, 21 October 2019
1727;   Tuesday, 22 October 2019
1708;   Wednesday, 23 October 2019
1717;   Thursday, 24 October 2019
2021;   Friday, 25 October 2019
0712;   Saturday, 26 October 2019; Rainy Day in Memphis . . .
1112;   Sunday, 27 October 2019
1710;   Monday, 28 October 2019
2133;   Tuesday, 29 October 2019
1859;   Wednesday, 30 October 2019
1902;   Thursday, 31 October 2019
1750;   Friday, 01 November 2019; Let Your Light from the Lighthouse Shine on Me!
0230;   Saturday, 02 November 2019
0837;   Sunday, 03 November 2019; Daylight Saving Time, fall back . . .
1732;   Monday, 04 November 2019
1744;   Tuesday, 05 November 2019
1916;   Wednesday, 06 November 2019
1926;   Thursday, 07 November 2019; Last night, I when to Merton Avenue Baptist Church for Bible Study for the 1st time where Ezell Owens is the Pastor. Bro. Larry spoke on "Never Lose Hope," and it was

heartfelt. Pastor E. Owens asked me to teach next Wednesday night Bible Study. Glory be to God!

0701; Saturday, 09 November 2019

0628; Sunday, 10 November 2019

0421; Monday, 11 November 2019; Veterans Day!

1844; Tuesday, 12 November 2019

1826; Thursday, 14 November 2019; Wednesday the 13th was my Bible Study night to speak on "True Friends," which was the topic. I pray it went well; I feel I could have presented it better. Glory Be To God!

1749; Friday, 15 November 2019

0651; Sunday, 17 November 2019

1807; Monday, 18 November 2019

1731; Tuesday, 19 November 2019

1757; Wednesday, 20 November 2019

1714; Thursday, 21 November 2019

1914; Friday, 22 November 2019

0600; Saturday, 23 November 2019

0518; Sunday, 24 November 2019

1739; Monday, 25 November 2019

1840; Wednesday, 27 November 2019

0652; Thursday, 28 November 2019; Happy Thanksgiving Day

0418; Friday, 29 November 2019

2037; Sunday, 01 December 2019; Hallelujah! I had a wonderful time at my cousin Georgia's birthday party yesterday evening at the Courtyard Marriot in Columbus, Mississippi; she turned a "fabulous 56." Today, before my son and I returned home, we visited Bro. R. Carter in Louisville, Mississippi; his hospitality was so very welcoming. We engaged in conversation, laughed, and watched a little of the Titans and Colts' game together. When my son Alvin and I left to travel back to Memphis, Tennessee, the score was 14 (Titans) and 17 (Colts), but the score ends up being 31 (Titans) and 17 (Colts); Tennessee Titans Triumph . . . Hooray!

2156; Monday, 02 December 2019

1937; Wednesday, 04 December 2019

1710; Thursday, 05 December 2019

1746; Friday, 06 December 2019

0422; Saturday, 07 December 2019

0752; Sunday, 08 December 2019; Nice Chilly Day. I'm going to look over a few things in the book, drop my bills in the mailbox, and ride over to Little Rock to visit my older sister for a day. When I return late this evening, I will finish preparing the book to be sent to AuthorHouse for tomorrow, hopefully. Early this morning, Father God placed in my spirit to add people to the Acknowledgement Page, not just Him; that's what I'm working on before I leave. In brief, I have been praying concerning the next book to write about for the last week; nothing has been revealed to me at this time. I also prayed concerning this book, whether I have left anything out, have I made the chapters clear, do I need to expound on any chapter more, and is it ready to be sent to AuthorHouse this coming week. As I got back into my bed and laid down, the unction of the Holy Spirit said, "Oasis." The word "Oasis" has many meanings. I prefer the meaning "a small fertile spot, in a desert, where a spring of water is found."

2033; Monday, 09 December 2019; Tonight, is the night. Praise God!

PREFACE

Isaiah 26:3-4, "Perfect Peace XX" Judges 4:1 – 16

The book <u>Isaiah 26:3-4, "Perfect Peace XX" Judges 4:1 – 16,</u> is the 20th book in a series called Isaiah 26:3-4, "Perfect Peace." Hallelujah!

It all started from how I drew near to the LORD in my workplace by keeping my mind on Him. I related numbers you see throughout the day, everywhere, on almost everything on Him, His word, biblical events, and facts to give me peace in the midst of chaos.

It's our desire for you to discover the power of the Holy Spirit by numbers, words, places, people, and things surrounding the biblical event recorded in "Judges 4:1 – 16."

Remember, the LORD Jesus <u>PROMISED us TRIBULA-TION</u> while we were in this world.

These things, I have spoken unto you,
that in me ye might have peace.
In the world ye shall have tribulation:
But be of good cheer; I have overcome the world.
John 16:33 KJV

However, we have been <u>PROMISED His PEACE</u> while we endure these trials, tribulations, troubles, and tests. Perfect Peace is given only to those whose mind and heart reclines upon the LORD. God's peace is increased in us according to the knowledge of His Holy Word.

> **Grace and peace be multiplied unto you**
> **through the knowledge of God,**
> **and of Jesus our LORD.**
> 2 Peter 1:2 KJV

Thanks . . . *To the Readers of the World*

As a disciple of the LORD Jesus Christ, I have learned true success comes when we are seeking and striving to do God's purpose for our lives. Our real happiness lies in doing God's will, even in the midst of our trials, tests, temptations, and tribulations; but not in fame and fortune.

Note of Interests: Trials leave us with a stronger faith in God. **Tests** allow us to see whether we can apply the word of God to live a righteous life in a sinful world. How we handle our **temptations** is a good indicator of our spiritual development. **Tribulations** are ordeals that an individual goes through, cause mostly by persecution.

I appreciate your support. Thanks for helping me spread the "Perfect Peace Series" through your e-mail, Facebook, Twitter, LinkedIn, Instagram, Tumblr, Messenger, or other accounts to your family, friends, neighbors, co-workers, church family, internet social friends, and associates.

Remember, you may not know until you get to heaven just how much a song you sung, kind words spoken by you, a book you suggested reading, or gave as a gift, at the right moment, encourage that person to keep on going when a few minutes before they were tempted to give up on life and their walk with the LORD.

Your lovingkindness to this ministry is greatly appreciated.

ACKNOWLEDGEMENTS

I wish to express my sincere gratitude to "Our Heavenly Father" for his guidance, patience, and lovingkindness throughout the writing of this book.

I like to thank my oases during the writing of this book.

Prophet Daniel in Memphis, TN

AWE Conference, Louisville, KY

ARK Encounter Experience and Staff in Williamstown, KY

Merton Avenue Baptist Church in Memphis, TN

Cousin Georgia's Birthday Party Gathering in Columbus, MS

Bro. Raymond Carter in Louisville, MS

My Son, Alvin Jackson in Memphis, TN

Weekly Prayer Lines hosted by Bro. James from Atlanta, GA; Bishop G. Coleman from Starkville, MS; Apostle D. Smith from Sikeston, MO; Prophet C. Allen from Forest, MS; Pastor JoAnn from Indianapolis, IN; and Minister Von from San Antonio, TX

INTRODUCTION

For Those Who Want to Be Kept In "Perfect Peace"

This book titled, <u>Isaiah 26:3 – 4, "Perfect Peace XX" Judges 4:1 – 16</u> was prepared and written to open your mind to a "Perfect Peace" that comes only from God. I'm striving through this book to elevate you into a "Unique and Profound" awareness of God's presence around you at all times.

According to some people, it's hard to keep your mind on the LORD. While most Christians will agree that if you keep your mind stayed on the LORD, He will keep you in "Perfect Peace." Therefore, so many people enjoy going to church on Sundays and attending midweek services for the peace and joy that they receive; but only for a short time.

You can experience the peace of the LORD throughout the day and every day. His unspeakable joy, his strength, his "Perfect Peace" during the storm, whether it's at work, home, college, school, etc. You can also experience this peace, even when your day is going well.

This concept of this book was placed in my spirit by our Father, which art in heaven, to help me when he allowed Satan to test me at my workplace until he finished molding me into a MAP; (Minister/Ambassador/Pastor).

Throughout these pages, I will be focussing on biblical events and facts surrounding "Judges 4:1 – 16." However, I am sure much more can be said concerning "Judges 4:1 – 16," so these chapter subjects serve merely as an introduction and are not exhaustive by any means.

DEDICATION

This book is dedicated to all the Judges,
especially,
the female Judges in the World.

CHAPTER 1

THE BOOK OF JUDGES

The word "Bible" originated from the Greek word "Biblia," which means "books." Scholars describe the Bible as sacred writings of Judaism and Christianity. The Bible is comprised of 66 books, with 2 major sections. The 2 major sections of the Bible are called the Old Testament and the New Testament.

The first section of the Bible called the Old Testament was written originally in Hebrew, except for some portions was written in Aramaic. The Old Testament has a collection of 39 books with 4 major divisions. The first division is called the Books of Law, also known as the Pentateuch. The second division of the Old Testament is called Historical Books. The third division of the Old Testament is called Poetry, and the last division is called the books of the Prophets. The books of the Prophets are classified as Major and Minor.

Note of Interests: The Book of Malachi is the last book of the Old Testament. There were approximately 400 years before the writing of the Book of Matthew, the first book of the New Testament. Those 400 years are called the "silent years."

The second section of the Bible is called the New Testament was originally written in Greek. The New Testament records the life of Jesus and the beginning of Christianity. The New Testament has 27 books, with 5 major categories, which are called the Gospels, Church History, Pauline Epistles, General Epistles, and Prophecy.

The Book of Judges is also merely called "Judges." It is the 7th book in the Old Testament and the 2nd book of the Deuteronomic History.

Question: What is the 7th book in the New Testament?

Smile
Answer in the back of the book.

The Book of Judges belongs to a specific historical tradition called the Deuteronomic History, which were 1st committed to writing during the Babylonian Exile around 550 BC. Five books belong to the Deuteronomic History, the other 4 books are Deuteronomy, Joshua, 1st and 2nd Samuel, along with 1st and 2nd Kings.

Note of Interests: The books of 1st Samuel and 2nd Samuel, along with 1st Kings and 2nd Kings were a single book, and still are in some Jewish Bibles.

The Book of Judges doesn't indicate who wrote the book. However, Jewish tradition names the prophet Samuel as the author. The Book of Judges covers approximately 300 years, and those years begin after the conquest described in the Book of Joshua. Those 300 years described Judges that ruled over Israel and biblical events that occurred up to the establishment of the kingdom in the books of Samuel.

Biblical Judges presided over the affairs of the Israelites. Judges were individuals who served roles as military leaders in times of crisis. They were chosen by God to rescue the people from their enemies, establish justice, and solve legal issues among the people. It was during the interval between the death of Joshua and the accession of the first King, Saul. God established them before the Israelite monarchy.

The Book of Judges focuses on the Israelites idolatry, failures, and God abiding mercy. Throughout the Book of Judges, there is a cycle of rest, relapse, ruin, repentance, restoration, deliverance, and peace for God's chosen people; the Israelites.

The Book of Judges mentions 12 individuals who judged Israel, which were **Othniel**, **Ehud**, Shamgar, **Deborah**, **Gideon**, Tola, Jair, **Jephthah**, Ibzan, Elon, Abdon, and **Samson**. Othniel, Ehud, Deborah, Gideon, Jephthah, and Samson are known as the 6 significant judges out of the 12 judges.

Note of Interests: Other Judges mentioned in the Bible were Joshua, Abimelech, Eli, and Samuel.

The 1st chapter of Judges opens with the Israelites in the land of Canaan, the land that God has promised to them. The Book of Judges can be divided into 2 sections:

<u>Introduction and The Judges of Israel, Chapters 1 – 16</u>

1. Introduction and Israel Fights the Remaining Canaanites, Judges 1:1 – 3:6
2. Othniel, Judges 3:7 – 11
3. Ehud, Judges 3:12 – 30
4. Shamgar, Judges 3:31
5. Deborah and Barak, Judges 4:1 – 5:31
6. Gideon Judges 6:1 – 8:35
7. Tola, Judges 10:1 – 2
8. Jair, Judges 10:3
9. Jephthah, Judges 10:6 – 12:7
10. Ibzan, Judges 12:8 – 9
11. Elon, Judges 12:11 – 12
12. Abdon, Judges 12:13 – 15
13. Samson, chapters 13 – 16

<u>Sins, Chapters 17 – 21</u>

1. Micah's Idol and the Danites, chapters 17 – 18
2. The Levites Concubine and the Battle at Gibeah, chapters 19 – 21

Note of Interests: The phrase "the children of Israel <u>did evil</u> in the sight of the LORD" is only mentioned 3 times in the KJV, and only in the Book of Judges; Judges 2:11, Judges 3:7, and Judges 6:1. Judges 4:1 says, "the children of Israel <u>again did evil</u> in the sight of the Lord." Judges 3:12, Judges 10:6, Judges 13:1 says, "the children of Israel <u>did evil again</u> in the sight of the Lord." Other individuals in the Bible, "who did evil in the sight of the Lord" are listed below.

1. Solomon, the 3rd and last king when Israel was a United Kingdom,1 Kings 11:6
2. Rehoboam, King of Judah, 1 Kings 14:21 – 22
3. Nadab, King of Israel - 1 Kings 15:25 – 26
4. Baasha, King of Israel - 1 Kings 15:33 – 34
5. Ahab, King of Israel - 1 Kings 16:30
6. Ahaziah, King of Israel - 1 Kings 22:51 – 52
7. Jehoram, King of Judah - 2 Kings 8:16 – 18

The last verse in the Book of Judges reads, also follow, and a similar verse is also mentioned in Judges 17.

In those days there was no king in Israel:
every man did that which was right in his own eyes.
Judges 21:25 KJV

In those days there was no king in Israel,
but every man did that which was right in his own eyes.
Judges 17:6 KJV

CHAPTER 2
JUDGES 4:1 - 16

The Book of Judges or Judges has 21 chapters. However, chapter 4 contains the "passage of scripture," which inspired this book. The 4th chapter of Judges has 24 verses, and the words which are in **bold print** will be discussed in the chapters to follow.

Note of Interests: The phrase "passage of scripture" means a segment, section, piece, or portion of a written work; in this case, the KJV Bible. The word "scripture" is defined as the sacred writings of the Old and New Testaments. Some scholars believe one of the best ways to study a "passage of scripture" is by observation, interpretation, and application. First, read the "passage of scripture," observing what the written word says. Next, is the interpretation, which is understanding the meaning of that "passage of scripture." Lastly, is the application, after the "passage of scripture" has been observed, and interpreted, apply it to our heart, mind, soul, and body. Then the "passage of scripture" should encourage, strengthen, motivate, teach, and reveal knowledge to our lives through the LORD.

Let's read this "passage of scripture" four times, slowly in the name of Jesus. May the LORD bless the readers, hearers, and doers of His Word.

<u>Deborah</u>, Israel's 4th Judge

And the **children of Israel** again did evil in the sight of the LORD, when **Ehud** was dead.

And the LORD sold them into the hand of **Jabin king of Canaan**, that reigned in **Hazor**; the captain of whose host was **Sisera**, which dwelt in **Harosheth of the Gentiles**.

And the children of Israel cried unto the LORD: for he had nine hundred **chariots of iron**; and twenty years he mightily oppressed the children of Israel.

And Deborah, a prophetess, the wife of Lapidoth, she judged Israel at that time.

And she dwelt under **the palm tree** of Deborah between **Ramah and Bethel** in mount Ephraim: and the children of Israel came up to her for judgment.

And she sent and called **Barak** the son of Abinoam out of **Kedeshnaphtali**, and said unto him, Hath not the LORD God of Israel commanded, saying, Go and draw toward **mount Tabor**, and take with thee 10,000 men of the children of **Naphtali** and of the children of **Zebulun**?

And I will draw unto thee to the **river Kishon** Sisera, the captain of Jabin's army, with his chariots and his multitude; and **I will deliver him** into thine hand.

And Barak said unto her, If thou wilt go with me, then I will go: but if thou wilt not go with me, then **I will not go**.

And she said, **I will surely go** with thee: notwithstanding the journey that thou takest shall not be for thine honour; for **the LORD shall** sell Sisera into the hand **of a woman**. And Deborah arose, and went with Barak to Kedesh.

And Barak called Zebulun and Naphtali to Kedesh; and he went up with 10,000 men at his feet: and Deborah went up with him.

Now **Heber the Kenite**, which was of the children of **Hobab** the father in law of Moses, had severed himself from the Kenites, and pitched his tent unto **the plain of Zaanaim**, which is by Kedesh.

And they shewed Sisera that Barak the son of Abinoam was gone up to mount Tabor.

And Sisera gathered together all his chariots, even 900 chariots of iron, and all the people that were with him, from Harosheth of the Gentiles unto the river of Kishon.

And Deborah said unto Barak, Up; for **this is the day** in which the LORD hath delivered Sisera into thine hand: is not **the LORD** gone out before thee? So, Barak went down from mount Tabor, and 10,000 men after him.

And **the LORD discomfited** Sisera, and all his chariots, and all his host, with **the edge of the sword** before Barak; so that Sisera lighted down off his chariot and fled away on his feet.

But Barak pursued after the chariots, and after the host, unto Harosheth of the Gentiles: and all the host of Sisera fell upon the edge of the sword; and there was **not a man left**.

PS: The above scriptures were taken from the King James Version; KJV.

CHAPTER 3

DEBORAH

The name "Deborah" is mentioned 10 times in the KJV Bible. It refers to two women, one was a nurse, and the other was a judge. Deborah, who was a nurse, is only mentioned once in the Book of Genesis. Deborah, the judge, is mentioned 9 times, only in the Book of Judges.

Deborah in the Book of Genesis is spoken of as the nurse of Rebekah. According to Genesis 35:8, Deborah accompanied Rebekah from the house of Bethuel. Rebekah's nurse is only mentioned by name regarding her burial under the oak tree of Bethel, which was called in her honor Allonbachuth.

But Deborah, Rebekah's nurse died,
and she was buried beneath Bethel under an oak:
and the name of it was called Allonbachuth.
Genesis 35:8 KJV

Note of Interests: The word "Allonbachuth" is also spelled Allon-bachuth, Allon Bakuth, Allon-bacuth, Allon Bacuth, which means "oak of weeping."

There is no more history recorded concerning Deborah. Scholars believe that Deborah probably breast-fed Rebekah, when she was an infant because the word "nurse" means to "suckle." When Rebekah left home to be with her husband, Isaac, Deborah, her nurse went with her, Genesis 24:59 – 61.

Question: Who was Isaac's parents?

Smile
Answer in the back of the book

Now, Deborah, the judge of Israel, judged Israel for 40 years, between 1107 until her death in 1067 BC. She was the 4th Judge of Israel, and her name is mentioned a total of 9 times in Judges 4 and 5; Judges 4:4, Judges 4:5, Judges 4:9, Judges 4:10, Judges 4:14, Judges 5:1, Judges 5:7, Judges 5:12, and Judges 5:15.

Note of Interests: The individuals who ruled and judged over the Israelites were called "mishpat," which means "judges." The titled and office of "judges" can be traced back to a time when Moses appointed assistants to help him resolve disputes among the Hebrews, Exodus 18. The Judges would seek guidance from God through prayer and meditation before making a ruling of matters concerning a dispute of issue that occurred among the people. The word "Mishpat" is now the modern Hebrew word for "law." A mishpatan is a lawyer. The Israel civil courts are called "batei mishpat Ishalom," which means "courts for making peace between people."

Deborah is best known for her role in the war against Jabin, the king of Canaan. She encouraged Barak to form an army, and together they destroy the army of the Canaanite, whose Commander was Sisera. After the victory, Deborah and Barak sang words of praise to God; Judges, chapter 5.

Deborah was also a prophetess who heard from God and spoke prophecies. She arbitrated disputes and spoke judgments among the people, Judges 4:5. She was a strong leader, who spoke encouraging words, as well as gave decisive commands that included summoning and commissioning Barak the general of Israel's army, Judges 4:6 – 14.

Deborah was indeed a remarkable judge, a military strategist, a poet, and a prophetess. She is one of the 5 righteous women designated as a "Prophetess" in the Bible. The other 4 righteous Prophetesses are listed below.

1. Miriam, Exodus 15:20
2. Isaiah's wife, Isaiah 8:3
3. Huldad, 2 Kings 22:14
4. Anna, Luke 2:36.

The two false prophetesses named in the Bible are Jezebel, Revelation 2:20, and Noadiah, Nehemiah 6:14.

The name "Deborah" means "bee," and it was a popular name among the Puritans. The name "Deborah" was 1st used by English Christians after the Protestant Reformation.

Note of Interests: The Protestant Reformation is often referred to as the Reformation. It was a widespread movement which began in 1517 to reform the Catholic Church in Western Europe. A German monk named Martin Luther was disturbed with the corruption and practices he saw within the Catholic Church. He nailed his ninety-five grievances against the Catholic Church on a chapel door in

Wittenberg, Germany. His action became the catalyst that led to Protestant Reformation.

⎯⎯⎯◆◆◆◆◆⎯⎯⎯

The word "bee" is mentioned once, only in the Old Testament, Isaiah 7:18.

> **And it shall come to pass in that day,**
> **that the LORD shall hiss for the fly that is in**
> **the uttermost part of the rivers of Egypt, and**
> **for the bee that is in the land of Assyria.**
> Isaiah 7:18 KJV

The word "bees" is mentioned 3 times in the Old Testament only; Deuteronomy 1:44, Judges 14:8, and Psalm 118:12. The word "bee" is used metaphorically in Isaiah 7:18, and the word "bees" is used metaphorically in Deuteronomy 1:44, and Psalms 118:12. Judges 14:8 is actually describing a bees.

> **After a time, he (Samson) returned to take her,**
> **and he turned aside to see the carcase of the lion:**
> **and, behold, there was a swarm of bees**
> **and honey in the carcase of the lion.**
> Judges 14:8 KJV

In Deuteronomy 14, the word "bees" is describing the Amorites pursuing the Israelites. According to Psalms 118, the word "bees" is describing the enemy nations that are surrounding the psalmist. In Isaiah 7, the word "bees" is describing the Assyrians invading agents of divine retribution. Bees in the land of ancient Israel were known to be aggressive.

Note of Interests: Bees operate within a complex colony. They can only function as a society. There is no such thing as a solitary bee that makes honey on its own. Instead, the bee is a creature that ventures about and does an ordinary job for the whole hive. Bees help flowers reproduce, make sweet honey, speak a language among each other, care for their offspring, armed and ready to protect the Queen Bee.

Even though bee(s) are mentioned only 4 times, what they produce is mentioned 56 times in various manners. Bees are the producer of honey, and honey was recognized as a great source of strength, 1 Samuel 14:27. John the Baptist ate locust and honey in the wilderness, Matthew 3:4.

Canaan was known as the land flowing with milk and honey, Exodus 3:8. The judgments of the Lord, as well as his words, were deemed sweeter than honey, Psalm 19:10, Psalm 119:103. Ezekiel tastes a scroll that was given to him by the Word of God, and it tasted sweet as honey, Ezekiel 3:3. The angel had John on the island of Patmos to eat a little book that was sweet as honey, Revelation 10:9 – 10.

CHAPTER 4

CHILDREN OF ISRAEL

The phrase "children of Israel" is used in both the Old Testament and the New Testament. The phrase is recorded over 600 times in the KJV Bible. It is mentioned in 586 verses in the Old Testament, and 14 verses in the New Testament. The phrase "children of Israel" is even mentioned 5 times in one verse; Numbers 8:19.

**And I have given the Levites as a gift
to Aaron and to his sons from among
the <u>children of Israel</u>,
to do the service of the <u>children of Israel</u> in
the tabernacle of the congregation,
and to make an atonement for the <u>children of Israel</u>:
that there be no plague among the <u>children of Israel</u>,
when the <u>children of Israel</u> come
night unto the sanctuary.**
Numbers 8:19 KJV

The phrase "children of Israel" is mentioned in each of the 5 books of Moses, which are Genesis, Exodus, Leviticus, Numbers, and Deuteronomy. The phrase emphasizes the lineage of the Hebrew people as being through the patriarch Jacob.

The "children of Israel" are also called "Israelites," the descendants of Abraham, Isaac, and Jacob. The history of the Israelites commences with God's covenant with Abraham in approximately 2000 BC, "I will make you into a great nation," Genesis 12:2. God made a promise to one man named Abraham, who was childless with his wife, Sarah.

Note of Interests: When God promised Abraham, He would make him a great nation; God also promised to bless all people through that nation. According to Genesis 12:3, Israel was a channel for God's blessings to all mankind, and it reads, **"And I will bless them that bless thee and curse him that curseth thee; and in thee shall all families of the earth be blessed,"** Darby.

According to Genesis 21:1 – 3, God miraculously provided a son to Abraham and Sarah, who was named Isaac, to fulfill the promise, Genesis 21:1 – 3. God repeated the father's promise to his son, Isaac, Genesis 26:1 – 6.

Note of Interests: Abraham was 100 years old when Isaac was born, and his wife, Sarah, was 90 years old. God also promised Abraham that his son by Sarah's handmaid named Hagar, would be a nation because he is his seed, Genesis 21:12 – 13.

Abraham's son, Isaac, married Rebekah when he was 40 years old. They were childless for 20 years until God opened her womb. Isaac and Rebekah had twin sons, who they named Esau and Jacob, Genesis 25:26. God then reaffirmed the covenant with Jacob, Genesis 28:13 – 15. According to Genesis 35:10, God changed Jacob's name to Israel, and at this time, Jacob had 11 sons, and Rachel was pregnant with Benjamin, Genesis 35:10.

Jacob 12 sons carried on the family lineage forming the 12 tribes of Israel. Jacob's 12 sons are named Reuben, Simeon, Levi, Judah, Dan, Naphtali, Gad, Asher, Issachar, Zebulun, Joseph, and Benjamin. The descendants of Jacob are collectively called the "children of Israel." The phrase "children of Israel" became the most common term for the Hebrews; the Israelites in the Bible.

God, who formed the nation of Israel, has been faithful to keep His promises to the sons of Abraham, Isaac, and Jacob. God's awesome power has been shown throughout Israel's history. The history of the children of Israel is recorded in the Bible as a continuing cycle of blessing and punishment for their obedience and disobedience to God's law.

The 1st reference to the phrase "children of Israel" is in Genesis 32, and there Jacob's life experience with God is mentioned, which led to his name changed from Jacob to Israel. The name "Israel" means "one who fights victoriously with God" or "a prevailing prince with God." It's the new name God gave Abraham's grandson Jacob after he withstood a spiritual struggle at Jabbok River, Genesis 32:22 - 32.

Now, at this point, the descendants of Abraham, Isaac, and Jacob are often referred to as the "children of Israel." In verse 32, the phrase "children of Israel" is mentioned for the 1st time.

**Therefore, the children of Israel eat
not the sinew of the shrank,
which is upon the hollow of the thigh, unto this day:
because he touched the hollow of Jacob's
thigh in the sinew that shrank.**
Genesis 32:32 KJV

Note of Interests: The phrase "children of Jacob" is mentioned 3 times in the Bible, referring to "children of Israel." In 2 Kings 17:34, the phrase "children of Jacob," refers to the account of Jacob's name change. In 1 Chronicles 16:13, and Psalm 105:6, the phrase "children of Jacob" is speaking on the same matter; the lineage of the "children of Jacob." Psalm 105:6 goes back farther with the Hebrew lineage, and it reads as follows, **"O ye seed of Abraham his servant, ye children of Jacob, his chosen.** While 1 Chronicles 16:13 reads, **"O ye seed of Israel his servant, ye children of Jacob his chosen ones."** Jacob (Israel) is the grandson of Abraham.

Abraham and his descendants relied on that promised, for more than 400 years, even during a period of slavery in Egypt. God delivered the Israelites out of Egypt in the Book of Exodus by a series of amazing and miraculous events. The Exodus out of Egypt is when the Jews acknowledge this act as the initiation of the nation of Israel.

Once the Exodus was completed, God established a conditional covenant with the Israelites at the Mountain of Sinai. It is there God proclaimed His Law; The Ten Commandments, Exodus 20. It is there God promises Israel blessings for adherence to His Law and curses for noncompliance.

Israel was destroyed by the Romans in 70 AD, and at that time, the Jews scattered throughout the whole world. The Jews eventually returned to the chosen land God gave to them. In 1948, over 1900 years later, Israel was once again a sovereign nation and re-established in the Promised Land. In 1967, the Jews retook Jerusalem. Through a series of miraculous events, the fulfillment of prophecy concerning God's chosen people has taken place.

CHAPTER 5

EHUD

The named Ehud has two meanings, which are "Unity," and the other one is "Glory." Ehud, the son of Gera, is mentioned in the Book of Judges 7 times. He was a judge, who was sent by God to deliver the Israelites from Moabite slavery and subjugation. Ehud or Ehud ben-Gera is described as left-handed, and a member from the Tribe of Benjamin.

Note of Interests: The Bible only mentioned 3 left-handed people, and they are from the Tribe of Benjamin. However, the name "Benjamin" means "son of my right hand." The 3 left-handed people mentioned in the Bible are Ehud, who assassinated the Moabite king, Judges 3:21; the 700 Benjamites who were accurate sling stone-throwers, Judges 20:16; and the 24 ambidextrous warriors who came to support David in Hebron, 1 Chronicles 12:2.

Ehud was the 2nd of the 12 judges between 1400 – 1350 BC, who led the Israelites during a time of need. The 1st judge was Othniel and the most famous judge was Samson, and his story is used to conclude the Book of Judges.

The Moabites had oppressed the Israelites for 18 years by the time they finally cried out to God for help and repented of their sins. In response, God raised Ehud to deliver Israel from their oppression. According to Judges 3:12 – 30, Ehud was sent to the Moabite King Eglon to deliver the Israelites annual tribute. Ehud made a small double-edge sword about 18 inches long and attached it on his right thigh under his clothes because he was left-handed. Most soldiers in Bible days kept their weapons on their left thighs, which made it easy for them to draw out with their right hand. Ehud was left-handed, and when he was checked for weapons, his small sword was missed because it was on his right thigh.

Ehud and his traveling companions came to King Eglon with Israel's annual tribute, which they were forced to pay. Ehud sent away the people who carried the tribute, and he returned to the king alone. Ehud asked Elgon could he speak with him in private, claiming he had a secret message for him from God. Eglon was intrigued and unafraid, believing Ehud to be unarmed, he dismissed his attendants and palace guards.

Afterward, Ehud said, "I have a message from God for you," Judges 3. Ehud immediately drew his sword and stabbed the king in the abdomen. When Ehud stabbed the king, the entire sword, which was about 18 inches long, including the handle, disappeared into the wound, enclosed by Elgon's fat. Ehud locked the doors to the king's chamber and escaped through the porch.

The king's assistants returned and found the doors locked. They assumed the king was using the bathroom, and they didn't want to disturb him. Eventually, they realized something was wrong. Once they unlocked the door, they found King Elgon dead.

Ehud quickly made his way back to Israel territory. He arrived at the town of Seraiah in Ephraim, and there Ehud sounded the horn and rallied the Israelite tribes. The Israelites were able to defeat the kingless Moabites. Israel block-off the fords of the Jordan River, and invaded Moab itself, killing about 10,000 Moabite soldiers.

Note of Interests: The Jordan River is about 156 miles long, and it flows north to south from the Sea of Galilee to the Dead Sea. The Jordan River had approximately 54 fords, in ancient times. A ford is a very shallow place in a stream or river where humans or animals can cross to the other side by walking across. The Romans were the 1st to construct bridges over the Jordan River.

———◆◆◆———

After the death of Eglon, and Israel's victory over the Moabites, Israel had peace in the land for 80 years, Judges 3:30.

Note of Interests: Once Israel was free from Eglon rule, the Israelites enjoyed 80 years of peace; this was the longest peaceful period recorded during the time of judges, Judges 3:30.

———◆◆◆———

CHAPTER 6

JABIN, KING OF CANAAN

The name "Jabin" originated from the Hebrew language, which means "wise," "one who is intelligent," "discerning." The Bible mentions two powerful kings named Jabin. They were kings of Canaan and fought battles against the Israelites. The first battle was fought at Merom led by Joshua, and the second battle was led by Deborah and Barak; Joshua 11 and 12, Judges 4 and 5.

The battles of Joshua and Deborah/Barak took place in the same era. However, Deborah and Barak's battle were the first battle to succeeded in overtaken the Canaanite's chariots of iron, which was 900, Joshua 4:13.

So, God subdued on that day Jabin the king of Canaan before the children of Israel.
Joshua 4:23 KJV

According to Joshua 11:1 – 23, the first king named Jabin lived at Hazor in the northern territory of Canaan. He organized an alliance with the northern kings against the Israelites, after hearing how Joshua and his armies had conquered and destroyed the fortified cities of the southern territory of Canaan.

Joshua attacked the allied forces by the waters of Merom, around 1448 BC. Jabin and his alliances were defeated, Jabin's city was burnt, and he was slain.

Note of Interests: Jericho was the 1st city to be conquered by the Israelites under Joshua. Jericho was the entrance to the heartland of Canaan. Jericho was surrounded by a tall, thick wall that was wide enough to have houses built on it.

According to Joshua 11, King Jabin allied forces were Jobab king of Madon, King of Shimrom, and the King of Achshaph. Jabin also sent messages to the kings who were in the northern hill country, and in the Jordan Valley south of Galilee, and the lowland. The king sent messages to Naphoth Dor heights of Dor in the west, to the kings of the Canaanites on the east and the west. Letters were delivered to the Amorites, Hittites, Perizzites, and the Jebusites in the mountains. Jabin even sent messengers to the Hivites, who lived at the foot of Mount Hermon in the land of Mizpah.

The armies of all these kings came out, as many people as the sand that is on the seashore, with their horses and chariots. They agreed to meet, and encamped together at the waters of Merom, to fight against Israel.

And the LORD said unto Joshua, Be not afraid because of them: for tomorrow about this time will I deliver them up all slain before Israel; thou hought their horses, and burn their chariots with fire, Joshua 11:6. Israel pursued the armies of Jabin and his alliances as far as Great Sidon, Misrephoth-maim, and the valley of Mizpeh to the east. They were struck down until there was no survivors.

Note of Interests: The great battle fought at Lake Merom was the last of Joshua's battles. Here for the 1st time the

Israelites encountered the iron chariots and horses of the Canaanites.

———◆◈◆◈◆———

Approximately 200 years later, another king of Hazor named Jabin, who was called "the king of Canaan," was defeated by Deborah and Barak during the time of Judges, Judges 4:1 – 23. He overpowered the Israelites and for 20 years, held them in subjection.

The Israelites were paralyzed with fear and gave way to downheartedness until Deborah and Barak aroused the nation Israel's spirit. Deborah summoned Barak, telling him what the LORD had commanded him to gather the tribes of Zebulun and Naphtali to go to Mount Tabor. Barak hesitated and said he would only go if Deborah went with him.

Deborah agreed, and because of Barak's lack of faith in God, she told him the acknowledgment of the victory would not go to him, but a woman. Deborah and Barak, with the help of 10,000 Israelites, gained a great victory over Jabin, Judges 4:10 – 16. The battle was called the "battle of Deborah," and it brought an end to the Canaanite city of Hazor and completed the conquest of Canaan.

Note of Interests: The battle of Deborah and Barak was the 1st great victory Israel had gained since the days of Joshua. Israel never had to fight another battle with the Canaanites, Judges 5:31.

———◆◈◆◈◆———

CHAPTER 7

HAZOR

The word "Hazor" is recorded in the KJV Bible 19 times in 17 verses, and only in the Old Testament. Hazor is mentioned the most in the Book of Joshua. The Book of Joshua is the 6th book in the KJV Bible. It is also the 1st book of the Deuteronomistic History, which records the biblical events surrounding Israel from the conquest of Canaan to the Babylonian exile.

The Book of Joshua details the movement, struggles, and battles of the Israelites in central, southern, and northern Canaan. Joshua describes the defeat of Israel's enemies and the division of their enemies' land among the 12 tribes of Israel.

Hazor is mentioned 10 times in the Book of Joshua in chapters 11, 12, 15, and 19. Joshua 11:10 and Joshua 15:25 mentions Hazor twice in the same verse.

**And Joshua at that time turned back, and took Hazor,
and smote the king thereof with the sword:
for Hazor beforetime was the head
of all those kingdoms.**
Joshua 11:10 KJV

**And Hazor, Hadattah, and Kerioth,
and Hezron, which is Hazor.**
Joshua 15:25 KJV

Hazor is also mentioned 3 times in the Book of Jeremiah, twice in Judges and then once in the following books of the Bible, 1 Samuel 12, 1 Kings 9, 2 Kings 15, and Nehemiah 11.

Hazor is pronounced "hah – zawr," and the name means "enclosed; fortified." Several dictionaries describe Hazor as an ancient city in Israel, 9 miles north of the Sea of Galilee, which at one time was the capital of the Canaanite kingdom. Biblical scholars believe that the name "Hazor" refers to 4 biblical places in the Bible.

The Hazor near Lake Merom, located on an ancient trade route from the north, east, and west, is the most well-known city name Hazor. During the time of Joshua, Hazor was a pagan Canaanite city, the capital of Canaan, a military stronghold of the Canaanites located in the mountains north of Lake Merom, Joshua 11:1 – 5.

Jabin, the king of Hazor with his league of northern Canaanite cites, encountered Joshua in a great battle there. Hazor was conquered and burned by Joshua, which was a significant victory, which virtually completed his conquest of Canaan, Joshua 11:10 – 13. Hazor was captured and burned by Joshua in his victory over a league of northern Canaanite cites at Lake Merom, Joshua 11:1 – 11.

Note of Interests: Hazor is the largest archaeological site in Israel. Hazor was a 200-acre city with an Upper City and the Lower City. Hazor was the next largest city, apart from Jerusalem.

According to Joshua 19:36, Hazor came under the ownership of the tribe of Naphtali. Then later, Hazor was retaken by the Canaanites.

According to Judges 4 and 5, Deborah delivered Israel from the oppression of the King of Hazor, King of Canaan, and his general Sisera. Hazor was once again part of the kingdom of Israel, and King Solomon fortified Hazor, 1 Kings 9:15.

Hazor was destroyed for the last time by Assyrian Tiglath-pileser III when he invaded the land in 733 BC, 2 Kings 15:29. The Israelites were taken captive to Assyria.

Note of Interests: Hazor was one of the 1st cities Tiglath-pileser captured.

CHAPTER 8

SISERA

The Book of Judges is where the name "Sisera" is mentioned the most. His name is pronounced "sis'-er-a," and the name means "one who contemplates." The name "Sisera" is mentioned 19 times, only in the Old Testament.

Scholars believe the name Sisera belongs to two men in the Bible. One is mentioned briefly in Ezra 2:53 and Nehemiah 7:55, as one of the Israelite exiles who were allowed to leave Babylon and returned back to their own land; Jerusalem and Judah. This Sisera served as a temple servant.

The other Sisera is mentioned 15 times in the Book of Judges, chapters 4 and 5, and once in 1 Samuel 12 and Psalm 83. He lived in the time of Judges and was the commander of a Canaanite army. The Canaanites King Jabin was the LORD's instrument to punish the Israelites for their idolatry, Judges 4. The Israelites cried out to the LORD for deliverance. Deborah, the prophetess, who was also judging at that time, received word from the LORD to summon Barak to prepare for battle against the Canaanites.

Judges 4:2 is the 1st place Sisera's name is mentioned.

**And the LORD sold them into the
hand of Jabin king of Canaan,
that reigned in Hazor;**

the captain of whose host was Sisera,
which dwelt in Harosheth of the Gentiles.
Judges 4:2 KJV

The Israelites destroyed Sisera and his alliance's armies. Sisera fled until he came to the dwelling of Heber, the Kenite, who was allied with King Jabin of Canaan. Sisera approached Heber's wife, who is named Jael. Jael promised Sisera safety in her tent, and he entered her tent to hide from Barak.

Sisera told Jael, he was thirsty, and she gave him some milk. She covered him with a blanket, and he fell fast asleep. While Sisera was sleeping, Jael took a tent-peg and hammer, sneaked up on the sleeping commander, and drove the tent-peg through his skull and into the ground, Judges 4:19 – 21.

Barak was searching for Sisera, Jael led him into the tent to show him Sisera's body with his head pinned to the ground. Deborah's prophecy that Sisera would be brought down by a woman was fulfilled.

On the day of Sisera's death, Deborah and Barak sang a song of praise, which is recorded in Judges 5:1 – 31. The song details the LORD deliverance of the Israelites from the hands of the evil commander, Sisera.

Israel triumph over Sisera and his army would be remembered and later pen in one of King David's psalms.

Assur also is joined with them:
they have holpen the children of Lot.
Selah

Do unto them as unto the Midianites;
as to Sisera, as to Jabin, at the brook of Kison:
Which perished at Endor: they
became as dung for the earth.
Psalm 83:8 – 10 KJV

CHAPTER 9

HAROSHETH OF THE GENTILES

The phrase "Harosheth of the Gentiles" refers to a nation of mixed races that inhabited a city north in the land of Canaan near Hazor in Galilee. According to Genesis 12:7, the land of Canaan was the land God promised to give Abraham and his descendants. The Canaanites were large and fierce people, and many of their cities were huge with towering walls. However, God promised Moses and Joshua divine help in their battles against them, so they could defeat them, take their land, and cities.

In brief, after the Israelites exodus Egypt, the LORD told Moses to invade Canaan. Moses sent 12 men to spy out the land of Canaan. The spies brought back fruits of the land. One cluster of grapes from the land was so huge it took 2 men to carry them back. The spies described the inhabitant as giants compared to the Israelites. At that time, the Israelites were afraid of the Canaanites and refused to go into the land God had promised them.

Only Joshua and Caleb were confident that God would help them defeat the Canaanites. Because of the Israelites lack of trust in God, God allowed that generation of Israelites to wander in the wilderness for 40 years until all of them died, except for Joshua and Caleb. After Moses died, Joshua was called by God to lead the people of Israel into Canaan, the Promised Land.

The Canaanites are described in the Bible in several verses. According to Genesis 9:18, the Canaanites were idolatry people descended from Noah's grandson Canaan, who was a son of Ham. The word "Canaanites" is used to refer to all the inhabitants of the land of Canaan, which included the Hivites, Girgashites, Jebusites, Amorites, Hittites, and Perizzites, Judges 1:9 – 10. According to Joshua 11:3, the Canaanites refers to the people of the lowlands and plains of Canaan.

However, Scholars believe the city of the "Harosheth of the Gentiles" stood on the west coast of the Lake Merom. It was at Lake Merom where Joshua had his last battle with the Canaanites.

Note of Interests: The "waters of Merom" or "Lake Merom" is supplied by the Jordan River. It was approximately 10 miles north of the Sea of Galilee, shaped similarly to a triangle about 4 ½ miles in length by 3 ½ miles in width. The Lake Merom is surrounded by marshland, which is thickly covered with canes and papyrus reeds. Lake Merom is also recorded as the 3rd and last victorious battle scene for Joshua over the Canaanites, Joshua 11:5 – 7.

Harosheth is pronounced "ha-rosheth," and it means "workmanship." It was the home of Sisera, the commander of Jabin King of Canaan's army. Harosheth is also the location where the enormous army of Jabin gather before it went forth into battle against Deborah and Barak, Judges 4:13.

**And Sisera gathered together all his chariots,
even nine hundred chariots of iron, and
all the people that were with him,
from Harosheth of the Gentiles
unto the river of Kishon.**
Judges 4:13 KJV

Note of Interests: The KJV used the phrase "Harosheth of the Gentiles," but other Bible Translations use the following words: Harosheth Haggoyim, Harosheth-haggoyim, Harosheth-Haggoyim, and Harosheth-Goim. Harosheth Haggoyim is described as a fortress or cavalrymen of Sisera, while Harosheth of the Gentiles describes the people who lived in that city.

⬧◆⬧◆⬧

According to Judges 4, Deborah and Barak were victorious over Sisera's army.

CHAPTER 10

CHARIOTS OF IRON

The phrase "chariots of iron" is mentioned only 4 times in the Bible. Once in the Book of Joshua and 3 times in the Book of Judges. The word "chariot" comes from the Latin word "carrus," means "four-wheeled baggage wagon."

A chariot is a type of carriage driven by a charioteer using horses, and some used oxen. Armies used chariots as transport and for a mobile archery platform. Chariots have been known to be used for hunting, racing, and as a conveniently fast way to travel for many ancient people.

The chariots were initially used for ancient warfare during the Bronze and Iron Ages. They were an open vehicle with two-wheeled conveyance drawn by two or more horses, hitched side by side. The chariot had a floor with a waist-high guard at the front and sides. Chariots eventually lost their military importance by the 1st century AD.

Note of Interests: The Bronze Age ended around 1200 BC when man began to forge an even stronger metal called "iron." The Iron Age followed the Bronze Age beginning in the Mediterranean Region and Near East. The Iron Age is the final era of the three-age division of the prehistory of humanity. The three-age division is the Stone Age, the Bronze Age, and the Iron Age.

The "chariots of iron" were an ancient horse-driven two-wheeled vehicle used mostly in war. Usually, a highly trained charioteer controlled the horses, while the warrior thrust spears on the enemy soldiers on the battlefield.

The phrase "chariots of iron" is mentioned in Joshua 17:16, Judges 1:19, Judges 4:3, and Judges 4:13. According to Joshua 17, a land allotment was made to the tribe of Manasseh, the firstborn of Joseph. When the children of Joseph saw what land they were given, they begin to complain to Joshua. The children of Joseph felt that they weren't given enough land for their people. Joshua told them to clear the wood country; then, they would have plenty of land. The children of Joseph replied, "the hill is not enough for us: and all the Canaanites that dwell in the land of the valley have chariots of iron," Joshua 17:16.

The second times "chariots of iron" is mention is Judges 1:19, and it reads as follow.

And the LORD was with Judah;
and he drave out the inhabitants of the mountain;
but could not drive out the inhabitants of the valley,
because they had chariots of iron.
Judges 1:19 KJV

The third and fourth time "chariots of iron" is mention is in Judges 4, referring to Sisera's 900 chariots of iron.

And the children of Israel cried unto the LORD:
for he had 900 chariots of iron;
and 20 years he mightily oppressed
the children of Israel.
Judges 4:3 KJV

> **And Sisera gathered together all his**
> **chariots, even 900 chariots of iron,**
> **and all the people that were with him,**
> **from Harosheth of the Gentiles**
> **unto the river of Kishon.**
> Judges 4:13 KJV

According to Judges 4, the people of Israel again did, what was evil in the sight of the LORD, after Ehud died. God sold Israel into the hand of Jabin king of Canaan because of their idolatry.

During 20 years of bondage, Israel tremble because of the 900 iron chariots of the Canaanites. The commander of those 900 fierce chariots were Sisera. Nine hundred chariots were a huge number of chariots in those days.

Note of Interests: When Pharaoh's soldiers pursued after Moses and his people at the Red Sea, he had only 600 chariots.

⸺⸺◆◆◆◆◆⸺⸺

The "chariots of iron" belonging to Sisera were more advanced than that of the Canaanites during Joshua's time. They were made of iron, and instead of being driven by 2 horses, each one was driven by as many as 10 horses. Each chariot carried a driver and 4 archers. There were pockets on the side of the chariots that were loaded with extra bows and hundreds of arrows. The chariots sides were ironclad, and long sharp blades rotated on the heavy wheels, so that the driver could drive over the enemy's foot soldiers, cutting them to pieces.

Note of Interests: The word "chariot" is often mentioned in the Old Testament by the prophets, as an instrument of war, a symbol of power and glory. Chariot is mentioned in 56 verses; and only 3 times in the New Testament in the Book of Acts, chapter 8.

CHAPTER 11

THE PALM TREE

Palm Trees are beautiful trees with unique features. There are over 2,500 species of palm trees. These species can be found throughout the world, from the sweltering desert to the tropical rainforest. The finest species of palm trees grew in Jericho, along the banks of the Jordan River, Deuteronomy 34:3.

The well-known palm trees are the Date Palm and Coconut Palm. The Palm Tree is called "Tamar" in Hebrew, which is viewed as more remarkable and beautiful than any other tree. The name "Tamar" was the name of several women in the Bible. Er's wife, David's daughter, and Absalom's daughter were named Tamar; Genesis 38:6, 2 Samuel 13:1, 2 Samuel 14:27.

Most palm trees have unbranched stems, with a slender straight trunk that rises to 100 ft in height. The palm trees have long taproots, which enable them to reach down to water sources not available to other plants and survive amid desert conditions.

Note of Interests: The tallest species of palm trees are the Quindio Wax Palm in Colombia. The tallest recorded palm tree grew 197 feet tall, which is about 18 ½ stories high. The Coco De Mer Palm Tree produces the largest seeds than any plant on earth located in Seychelles. The largest recorded seed weighed 66 pounds and were 20 inches in diameter.

―――――◈◆◈◆◈―――――

Palm trees have 2 different types of evergreen leaves; palmate and pinnate, which are arranged in a spiral shape at the very top of the palm tree trunk. The Palmate leaves look like hands and grow in a bunch at the end of a stem. The Pinnate leaves look like feathers and grow along either side of the stem.

The feathery, pale green leaves of the palm trees can reach from 6 to 20 feet long, drooping slightly at the end, bending from the top. The palm trees will begin to bear fruit after it has been planted between 6 to 8 years. Palm trees have been known to bear fruits for a century.

Palm trees provided many useful benefits for mankind. Coconuts are a product of palm trees, along with dates, betel nuts, and acai fruit, as well as palm oil. The dates from the palm trees grow below the leaves in clusters and are sweet to the taste.

The palm tree fruits were daily food for millions of people in Bible days. A vast majority of the inhabitants of Egypt, Arabia, and Persia lived almost entirely on its fruits. The palm trees had many medical benefits. The palm tree sap produced a delicious wine called "Kallu." The fibers of the base of the palm tree leaves were woven into ropes, straps, cords, and fasteners. The stalks and branches of the palm trees were used to make cages for animals, fences for gardens, and provided cooking oil. The palm's tall stem supplied timber, and its leaves were manufactured into bags, baskets, brushes, couches, mats, and lampstands. The camels fed upon the date stones of the palm tree fruits.

Palm trees have a deep history with humanity. Scholars believe it probably originated from the Fertile Crescent region, the "cradle of civilization" that extends between Egypt and Mesopotamia. Archaeological findings have shown that the date palm tree was used in Mesopotamian society. The whole land of Israel was called "the land of palms" by the Greeks and Romans Phoenicia.

In Judaism, palm trees represent peace and plenty. Roman Kings gave palm branches as a symbol of triumph to the triumphant champions of games and wars. Palm branches were used by the Jews as an emblem of victory and peace. The Assyrians and Egyptians considered the palm tree as "the tree of life." The palm tree was sacred to Ishtar and Astarte, as well as to Nut and Hathor.

Note of Interests: The Palm Trees that were once abundant in Judea is now relatively rare, except in the Philistine plain and Old Phoenician.

In the Bible, branches of the palm tree were carried at the feast of Tabernacle, Leviticus 23:40. Solomon carved all the walls of the temple with figures of cherubim, palm trees, and flowers, 1 Kings 6:29.

Note of Interests: Palm Trees are the only plants mentioned in the Bible as being in Heaven, Ezekiel 41:18, 19, 20, 26.

According to Matthew 21:7 – 9, at Jesus' triumphal entrance into Jerusalem sitting on an ass and a colt, a great multitude took palm branches and went out to meet him. They cried out, "Hosanna! Blessed is He that cometh in the name of the LORD." A tradition is now celebrated as Palm Sunday the week before Easter.

According to Psalm 92:12, "The righteous shall flourish like the palm tree: he shall grow like a cedar in Lebanon," KJV.

According to Revelation 7:9, the victory of all nations over the world, the devil, and the flesh are described as "clothed with white robes and palm branches in their hands."

CHAPTER 12

RAMAH AND BETHEL

Deborah, the fourth Judge of Israel, held court under a palm tree. The site was called the "Palm of Deborah," located between Ramah and Bethel in the hill country of Ephraim. There Deborah sits under a palm tree, and the children of Israel came up from the surrounding area for Deborah to judge issues between them.

The word "Ramah" means "high place." Ramah was a hilltop city in ancient Israel, located in the territory of Benjamin. The city was 1st mentioned in the Bible when Joshua allocated territory to the tribe of Benjamin after the conquest of Canaan, Joshua 18:25.

Samuel was born at Ramah around 1094 BC. He eventually made Ramah his home after spending his youth at the temple with the priest Eli at Shiloh, 1 Samuel 7:17. When the elders of Israel decided they wanted a king, they came to Ramah to request a king to Samuel, 1 Samuel 8:4 – 5.

According to 1 Samuel 19:18, around 1012 BC, David escaped from King Saul's court at Gibeah, and he sought refuge at Samuel's home in Ramah.

In 901 BC, the city of Ramah was enlarged and fortified by King Baasha of Israel as part of his vigorous campaign against King Asa of Judah. King Asa, in a counterattack, struck a treaty with Ben-Hadad, the King of Aram, who forced Baasha to retreat. King Asa then pull down the fortifications at Ramah, and the timber, planks, logs, and stones were used to build up his defenses near Geba in Benjamin, and Mizpah, 1 Kings 15:16 – 22.

The Babylonians destroyed Jerusalem in 587 BC. The captives were held at Ramah before they were deported to Babylon, Jeremiah 40:1. The prophet Jeremiah was amongst those who had been captured. Jeremiah wrote about his people mourning and bitter weeping in Ramah and Rachel, "crying for her children because her children are no more," Jeremiah 31:15.

Note of Interests: According to Matthew 2:17 – 18, the words "crying for her children because her children are no more," also mentioned when King Herod the Great massacred the infants of Bethlehem around 4 BC. King Herod was trying to kill the Messiah, baby Jesus.

The Bible speaks of two places named Bethel. The word "Bethel" means "House of God." One of the Bethel was a village in the Negev, it was one of the places where David sent spoils to his friends, and the elders of Judah, 1 Samuel 30:26 – 31.

Note of Interests: There are no specific geographical boundaries that define the Negev in the Bible. The Negev refers to the "dry land" south in the country of Israel. The nation of Israel was divided into 5 regions, which are the coastal plain, Shephelah the lowlands near the coast, Negev the dry land, the hill country, and the wilderness.

The other Bethel was an ancient city about 5 miles north of Ramah, located at the boundary between the tribes of Ephraim and Benjamin. The city of Bethel was a major trading center about 12 miles north of Jerusalem. Bethel's north-south road passed through Hebron in the south to Shechem in the north. Bethel's east-west road led from Jericho to the Mediterranean Sea, which was Bethel's most prominent road.

Note of Interests: Only Jerusalem is mentioned more than Bethel in the Old Testament. However, Bethel is not mentioned in the New Testament, like Jerusalem.

Bethel later became the border between the northern kingdom of Israel and the southern kingdom of Judah. Although Bethel was in the dry hill country, it had several natural springs, which supplied water in abundance.

Bethel is mentioned in 60 verses in the Old Testament. It is mentioned the most in Genesis and Joshua. Bethel is 1st mentioned in connection with Abram, who built an altar to God there, Genesis 12.

And he (Abram) removed from thence unto a mountain on the east of Bethel, and pitched his tent, having Bethel on the west, and Hai on the east:

and there he builded an altar unto the LORD,
and called upon the name of the LORD.
Genesis 12:8 KJV

According to Genesis 28, the city of Bethel was formerly named "Luz." Luz was renamed to "Bethel" by Jacob after he experienced an astounding dream there. While Jacob was traveling from Beersheba to Haran to escape his brother Esau, Jacob stopped for the night in Luz. Jacob fell asleep and dreamed of a ladder leading up to heaven from the earth. The angels of God were ascending and descending on the ladder, as God stood at the top, Genesis 28:10 - 13.

In Jacob's dream, God renewed his covenant promise to Jacob and promised that "all the families of the earth will be blessed" through his offspring. Jacob rose early in the morning and took the stone that he had used as his pillow, and set up an altar, and poured oil on top of it, and re-named the place "Bethel," which means "House of God."

The Ark of the Covenant was stationed at Bethel for a while and the people went there to seek God counsel during times of trouble, Judges 20. According to Genesis 35, Deborah, Rebekah's nurse, was buried under an oak tree near Bethel. Deborah, the judge of Israel, held court at a site between Ramah and Bethel.

During the time of the divided kingdom, King Jeroboam of Israel established two shrines for the northern kingdom to worship; one was at Bethel and the other at Dan. God sent prophets to preach and pronounce judgment and condemnation on Bethel because it was a place of wickedness and idolatry, 1 Kings 13, Amos 3, and Hosea 10.

On Elijah's last day on earth, he and Elisha encountered a company of prophets at Bethel, which confirmed Elijah's soon departure, 2 Kings 2.

When the northern kingdom of Israel fell captive under Assyrian around 740 BC, Bethel remained a house for priests, 2 Kings 17. King Josiah of Judah, around the 7th BC, destroyed Bethel's high places as part of his religious reforms, 2 Kings 23. Eventually, the city of Bethel was reduced to a small village.

Note of Interests: The area of Bethel is a town now occupied by the Palestinian. A tower marks the location where it's believed Jacob had the dream with the vision of the ladder leading up to heaven. Today, many nonconformist Christian chapels in Britain are called Bethel, which means "House of God."

CHAPTER 13
BARAK

The name "Barak" belongs to only one man in the Bible. The biblical event that surrounds his life is mentioned in the Book of Judges, chapters 4 and 5. Barak was the son of Abinoam from Kedesh in Naphtali, and his mother was from the tribe of Benjamin.

Note of Interests: The tribe of Benjamin was one of the 12 tribes of Israel. The tribe descended from the youngest son of the patriarch Jacob with his wife, Rachel. Benjamin was the only son of Jacob to be born in Canaan, and his mother died while giving birth to him near the Canaanite town known as Bethlehem, today. The tribe of Benjamin had 700 fighting men, who were left-handed, Judges 20:16. The tribe of Benjamin also had many distinguished slingers and archers, and one Benjamite named Ulam had 150 sons and grandsons who were expert archers. Ehud was from the tribe of Benjamin, a judge and a great warrior who delivered Israel from Moab, Judges 3:12 – 30. Saul, the 1st king of Israel, came from the tribe of Benjamin, 1 Samuel 9:15 – 27. According to Esther 2:5 – 7, Mordecai and Esther were from the tribe of Benjamin, they delivered their people, the Jews from a crisis that threatened their existence. In the New Testament, the Apostle Paul was from the tribe of Benjamin, Romans 11:1.

Barak means "lightning" in Hebrew, and he is mentioned in 13 verses in the Bible. Barak's name is mentioned 12 times in the Old Testament and once in the New Testament. In 2 chapters in the Book of Judges is where Barak's name is mentioned the most, and then once in the New Testament; the Epistle to the Hebrews, chapter 11.

Note of Interests: Barak's father, "Abinoam," name means "my father is pleasantness." Barak's father is mentioned in both the written account of Barak's victory over the Canaanites and in the song of Deborah and Barak in Judges 5:1 – 31.

Barak was described as a skilled military commander in the biblical Book of Judges. Barak, along with Deborah, led one of the greatest and the last battle of the Israelites over the northern Canaanite armies. However, this battle is known as the "battle of Deborah."

In brief, during the late 12 BC, Barak was reluctant to follow the LORD's command to go to war against the Canaanites. The Canaanites had 900 chariots of iron. Deborah sent for Barak and questioned him why he hasn't obeyed the LORD. Barak told Deborah that he wouldn't gather his forces against the Canaanites unless she would march with him. Deborah agreed to march with Barak, and he went back home to gather his army. Once he had his army of 10,000 men, they went to Tabor to confront the Canaanites. Barak's army was able to defeat the Canaanites, and not one of them remained.

The Epistle to the Hebrews, chapter 11, is often called the "Hall of Faith." The author of Hebrews 11 introduces a list of heroic individuals from the Old Testament who stood on God's faithfulness. Barak's faith is what gave him the victory over the Canaanites is mentioned in this list in the "Hall of Faith."

By faith the harlot Rahab perished not
with them that believed not,
when she had received the spies with peace.
And what shall I more say?
For the time would fail me to tell
of Gideon, and of Barak,
and of Samson, and of Jephthae; of
David also, and Samuel,
and of the prophets:
Who through faith subdued kingdoms,
wrought righteousness, obtained promises,
stopped the mouths of lions.
Hebrews 11:31 – 33 KJV

CHAPTER 14

KEDESHNAPHTALI

And she sent and called Barak the son of
Abinoam out of Kedeshnaphtali,
and said unto him,
Hath not the LORD God of Israel commanded, saying,
Go and draw toward mount Tabor,
and take with thee ten thousand men
of the children of Naphtali
and of the children of Zebulun?
Judges 4:6 KJV

The word "Kedeshnaphtali" is part of a 50-word verse in the Bible; Judges 4:6 KJV. The word is only mentioned once in the Bible, as the city where Barak lived. The word "Kedeshnaphtali" is also written in several formats depending on the Bible translation. The several ways the word "Kedeshnaphtali" is written in the above verse in the Bible are listed below, along with the Bible translation.

1. Kedeshnaphtali – KJV, NLV
2. Kedesh-naphtali – ASV, AMP, NASB
3. Kedesh-Naphtali – Darby
4. Kedesh Naphtali – WEB
5. Kedesh in Naphtali – NKJV, NIV, MSG
6. Barak lived in the city of Kedesh, which is in the area of Naphtali – ERV

The way in which, Kedeshnaphtali is expressed in the NKJV and ERV translations indicate that Kedesh was a city located in the territory of Naphtali.

Note of Interests: Naphtali was the 6th son of Jacob out of 12 sons. Naphtali's mother was named Bilhah, Rachel's handmaid. Jacob and Bilhah had two sons together, and the first son was named Dan. Jacob, his sons, and sons' families when down into Egypt, where his son, Joseph, was 2nd in command to the king of Egypt. Jacob's son named Naphtali had four sons, who were named Jahzeel, Guni, Jezer, and Shillem, which is the beginning of the Tribe of Naphtali.

———◆◆◆◆———

The word "Kedesh" is mentioned 11 times in the Bible, only in the Old Testament. Kedesh is mentioned in the books of Joshua (5), Judges (3), 2 Kings (1), and 1 Chronicles (2). The word "Kedesh" means "to be consecrated."

Some scholars believe there were 3 cities named Kedesh in the Bible. One city was in the far south of Judah; it was also known as Kedesh-barnea, Joshua 15:23. Another city named Kedesh was located in Issachar, 1 Chronicles 6:72. The city of refuge in Naphtali was called Kedesh; it was also known as Kedeshnaphtali, Joshua 19:37.

Kedesh was one of the six refuge cities named in the Bible. Kedesh was located on the west side of the Jordan River. The other 5 cities of refuge were Golan, Ramoth, and Bosor, on the east of the Jordan River, while Shechem and Hebron were on the west side.

The word "Naphtali" is mentioned 47 times, only in the Old Testament. The 1st place Naphtali is mentioned is in the Book of Genesis.

**And Bilhah Rachel's maid conceived again,
and bare Jacob a second son.
And Rachel said,
With great wrestlings have I wrestled
with my sister, and I have prevailed:
and she called his name Naphtali.**
Genesis 30:7 – 8 KJV

Kedeshnaphtali was one of the fortified cities of the tribe of Naphtali, between Hazor and Edrei, Joshua 19:37. It was appointed as a city of refuge and allotted towns to the Gershonite Levites, Joshua 21:32. Barak resides there, and there, he and Deborah assembled the tribes of Zebulun and Naphtali before the battle against the Canaanites in the late 12 BC.

Around 733 BC, Tiglath-pileser, king of Assyria, invaded Israel, and Kedeshnaphtali was captured. The captured took place during the reign of Pekah, the 18th King of Israel, 2 Kings 15:29.

CHAPTER 15

MOUNT TABOR

Mount Tabor played a significant role in Israel's history. The name "Tabor" means "clarify, purity." Mount Tabor is only mentioned in the Old Testament, a total of 10 times. Mount Tabor is mentioned 1st in Joshua 19, marking out the boundaries between the tribes of Issachar, Naphtali and Zebulun.

Mount Tabor, with its massive dome shape, can be seen from Jerusalem, about 97 miles away. Mount Tabor is 1,887 feet high, which is almost 19 stories high. Mount Tabor is located in the Valley of Jezreel; it's approximately 6 miles from Nazareth and 11 miles from the Sea of Galilee.

In the Book of Judges, Mount Tabor is the site of the battle between Israel's army and the Canaanites. Deborah, the Judge of Israel, summoned Barak to gather an army from the tribes of Naphtali and Zebulun at Mount Tabor. They descended from Mount Tabor to defeat Sisera, the commander of the Canaanite army, Judges 4:1 – 24.

Gideon avenged the death of his brothers, who were slain by the Midianite Kings on Mount Tabor, Judges 8:18 – 21. Psalm 89, a psalm of Ethan the Ezrahite, mentioned Mount Tabor and Mount Hermon in verses 12, as he praises and rejoices in God, verses 1 – 18.

The north and the south thou hast created them:
Tabor and Hermon shall rejoice in thy name.

Psalm 89:12 KJV

In the Book of Hosea, Mount Tabor is identified as one of the "high places" where the leaders of Israel set up altars for the worship of false gods, Hosea 5:1.

Note of Interests: In Bible days, especially in the Old Testament, it was believed that worshipping God on the top of mountains brought a person "closer to God." As a result, the Old Testament is filled with places that speak about altars built on "high places" to worship God, and false gods as well, 1 Kings 3:2, 1 Kings 12:32, 1 Kings 13:2, 1 Kings 14:23, 1 Kings 15:14, 1 Kings 22:43, 2 Kings 12:3, 2 Kings 14:4, 2 Kings 15:4, 2 Kings 17:11, 2 Kings 21:3, etc.

In Christian tradition, Mount Tabor is believed to be the place where Jesus' transfiguration occurred in Matthew 17. The mountain in which Jesus' transfiguration took place is not mentioned in the Bible. Some Scholars believe Mount Hermon is where Jesus' transfiguration took place because it's taller than Mount Tabor.

Question: Which disciples were with Jesus during his transfiguration?

Smile
Answer in the back of the book.

Emperor Constantine the Great's mother, Queen Helena, truly believed that Mount Tabor was the site of Jesus' transfiguration, and in 326 AD, she had the 1ˢᵗ church built on that mountain.

Note of Interests: In addition to the Biblical events that occurred on Mount Tabor, there are several events associated with Jesus and mountains, which are listed below.

1. The Sermon on the Mount, Matthew 5:1 – 7:29
2. The Great Commission, Matthew 28:16 – 20
3. The Feeding of the 5,000, John 6:3 – 14
4. Satan took Jesus to a "very high mountain," trying to tempt Him, Matthew 4:8 – 10, Luke 4:5 – 8
5. Jesus on several occasions went up a mountain for solitude and to pray, Matthew 14:23, Matthew 15:29, Mark 6:46, Luke 6:12 and John 6:15

A mountain is considered a natural elevation that rises at least 1,000 feet, which would be a little over 10 stories high by most scholars, and other scholars' states a mountain begins at 2,000 feet. However, a few important mountains regarding the Bible are listed below.

Mount Ararat is where Noah's ark came to rest upon 150 days after the flood began, Genesis 8:4.

Mount Moriah is where Abraham took Isaac to be a sacrifice, Genesis 22. Mount Moriah is also the place where Solomon built God's Temple. The Samaritans considered Mount Gerizim to be the same as Mount Moriah.

Mount Sinai, also called Mount Horeb, is where Moses received the Ten Commandments from God, Exodus 34:1.

Mount Nebo is where the LORD told Moses to go up to view the Promised Land, and he died and was buried there, Deuteronomy 34:1 – 8. Most scholars believe Mount Nebo and Mount Pisgah is the same mountain.

Mount Carmel is where Elijah challenged the prophets of Baal and was victorious, 1 Kings 18.

Mount Olivet is commonly known as the Mount of Olives. Mount of Olives is where Jesus delivers the "Olivet Discourse," Matthew 24 and 25. Mount Olivet is where Jesus went to pray before His crucifixion, and also where Jesus ascended into Heaven, Luke 22, and Acts 1.

Mount Seir is where Esau, the father of the Edomites dwell, Genesis 36:8.

Mount Gilboa is where Saul and his sons named Jonathan, Abinadab, and Malchishua were killed by the Philistines, 1 Samuel 31:2.

Mount Hor is the mountain where Aaron, the priest, died, Number 33:39.

Mount Zion eventually became known as Jerusalem, 2 Kings 19:31, Psalm 135:21, Hebrew 12:22.

CHAPTER 16

NAPHTALI

The name Naphtali means "struggle, wrestle." Naphtali is one of the 12 tribes that make up the nation of Israel. He was the 6th son of Jacob; Jacob was later renamed Israel by God. Naphtali was the younger of two sons born to Jacob by Bilhah, a maidservant of Jacob's 2nd wife named Rachel.

Naphtali had only one whole brother named Dan. He had 10 half-brothers, and one-half sister by his father, Jacob. A list of Jacob's children and Naphtali's brother, half-brothers and sister are listed below in the order they were born, along with their mother's name.

1.	Reuben	half-brother by Leah, Jacob 1st wife
2.	Simeon	half-brother by Leah, Jacob 1st wife
3.	Levi	half-brother by Leah, Jacob 1st wife
4.	Judah	half-brother by Leah, Jacob 1st wife
5.	Dan	brother by Bilhah, Rachel's maidservant
6.	Naphtali, the 2nd son of Bilhah, Rachel Maidservant	
7.	Gad	half-brother by Zilpah, Leah's maidservant
8.	Asher	half-brother by Zilpah, Leah's maidservant
9.	Issachar	half-brother by Leah, Jacob 1st wife
10.	Zebulun	half-brother by Leah, Jacob 1st wife

11.	Joseph	half-brother by Rachel, Jacob 2nd wife
12.	Benjamin	half-brother by Rachel, Jacob 2nd wife
13.	Dinah	half-sister by Leah, Jacob 1st wife

Naphtali had four sons when he traveled to Egypt with his father and relatives to live. Naphtali's sons were named Jahzeel, Guni, Jezer, and Shillem, which begins the development of the Tribe of Naphtali. The name of Naphtali's wife or wives is not given.

Note of Interests: When Jacob and his sons and sons' families when to Egypt, there were only 70 of them. When they came out of Egypt about 200 years later, there were about 600,000 of them.

According to Genesis 49, when Jacob blessed his sons just before he died, he described Naphtali as a deer that has been set free.

Naphtali is a hind let loose: he giveth goodly words.
Genesis 49:21 KJV

Moses led the people out of Egypt after the 10th plague that God sent on the land of Egypt. During those 200 years of living in Egypt, the people of Israel had been enslaved by the Egyptians.

During the march through the wilderness, Naphtali occupied a position on the north of the sacred tent with Dan and Asher, Number 2:25 – 31. Naphtali was one of 6 tribes chosen to stand on Mount Ebal and pronounce curses, Deuteronomy 27:13.

After Moses did, 40 years after the Exodus, Joshua led the people of Israel into the Promised Land of Canaan. Joshua divided the new territory among the 12 tribes. According to the Bible, Joshua assigned Naphtali, a region in northern Israel, northwest of the Sea of Galilee. Naphtali territory extended 800 square miles, twice as much land than Issachar.

The land of Naphtali was enclosed on 3 sides by the Tribe of Asher on the west, the Tribe of Zebulun on the south, and the Tribe of Manasseh on the east. It was located in a rich and fertile portion of northern Palestine.

Note of Interests: According to Genesis 30:8, when the census of the people was taken at Mount Sinai, Naphtali had 53,400 fighting men. When Naphtali had reached the Promised Land, they had been reduced to 45,4000 fighting men, Number 26:48 – 50.

Some of the events that occurred in the region of Naphtali are as follows. Barak, who commanded the army with Deborah, was from the region of Naphtali, Judges 4:6. In the Song of Deborah, the Tribe of Naphtali is praised for their bravery in defeating the Canaanite, Judges 5:18.

The Tribe of Naphtali, along with Manasseh, Asher, and Zebulun, aided Gideon against the army of the Midianites, Judge 6:35. According to Numbers 13:14, Nahbi the son of

Vophsi from the Tribe of Naphtali was one of the men, who was sent to spy out the land of Canaan.

When David was anointed and became king over all of Israel, the Tribe of Naphtali joined him in the town of Hebron with a large army, 2 Samuel 2:1 – 4. Around 922 BC, after the death of King Solomon, the son of King David, the Kingdom of Israel divided into two kingdoms; Israel and Judah. The 10 northern tribes established the Kingdom of Israel, and Naphtali was part of this kingdom.

Naphtali's territory was the 1st to suffer from the invasion of Benhadad, king of Syria, 1 Kings 15:20. In 734 BC, the descendants of Naphtali were conquered by the Assyrian king Tiglath-pileser III, whose armies in 721 BC gained control over the entire northern kingdom. The Israelites were deported into slavery, and those who remained behind gradually integrated with other people and adopted their cultures. The Tribe of Naphtali identity was lost and became known by Jewish legend, as one of the "Ten Lost Tribes of Israel."

Note of Interests: The southern portion of Naphtali's territory was called "the Garden of Palestine." Jesus started His public ministry in Naphtali. It was in the area of Galilee where Jesus called his 1st disciples from the shores of Galilee, Matthew 4:13 – 25. The land of Gennesaret, Bethsaida, Capernaum, and Chorazin lies within Naphtali boundaries. Jesus spoke most of his parables and performed many miracles in Naphtali's territory. The Tribe of Naphtali was called Nephtalim in Matthew 4:15. In Revelation 7,

Naphtali is among the tribes who are promised the seal of God for 12,000 of their members.

Naphtali is now a desert, except for the towns of Tiberias, on the shore of Lake Galilee, and Safed, the highest point in Galilee.

CHAPTER 17
ZEBULUN

The name "Zebulun" is of Hebrew origin, and it means "highly exalted." Zebulun was the 10th son of Jacob, and Jacob 6th and last son with Leah. Zebulun's brothers by his mother, and father, were Reuben, Simeon, Levi, Judah, and Issachar; he had one sister named Dinah. Zebulun had 6 half-brothers named Dan, Naphtali, Gad, Asher, Joseph, and Benjamin.

Zebulun is considered the father of the Israelite Tribe of Zebulun. Zebulun married Merushan, and they had 3 sons named Sered, Elon, and Jahleel. Zebulun's sons Sered became the father of the Saradites, Elon became the father of the Elonites, and Jahleel became the father of the Jahleelites, which enlarged the Tribe of Zebulun.

According to Genesis 49, Jacob gathered his sons and blessed them before he dies. Jacob said to Zebulun:

> **Zebulun shall dwell at the haven of the sea;**
> **and he shall be for a haven of ships; and**
> **his border shall be unto Zidon.**
> Genesis 49:13 KJV

According to the Book of Numbers, during the 2nd year of Israel Exodus from Egypt, a census of the tribes was taken in the Desert of Sinai. The descendants of Zebulun numbered 57,400 men fit for war, and the leader of the tribe was Eliab, son of Helon, Number 1:30 -31. The Tribe of Zebulun camped next to the tribes of Judah and Issachar, which was east of the Tabernacle, Numbers 2:3 – 9. When Moses sent out men to spy out the land of Canaan, Gaddiel, the son of Sodi was sent from the Tribe of Zebulun, Number 13. At Shittim, in the land of Moab after, 24,000 men died from a plague, a 2nd census was taken. The Zebulun at this census numbered 60,5000 fighting men, Numbers 26:27.

Note of Interests: In brief, the plague that killed 24,000 men at Shittim was sent by God. According to Numbers 25, the Israelites were camped at Acacia, and some of the men had sex with the Moabite women. They then offered sacrifices to their gods, ate the meat from the sacrifice, and worshiped the Moabite gods. The LORD became angry with Israel because they had worshiped the god of Baal Peor. God told Moses to have each man put to death who had worshiped Baal. The grandson of Aaron named Phinehas saw an Israelite man and a Midianite woman enters a tent. Phinehas took a spear and ran it through the man and woman. The LORD immediately stopped punishing Israel with a deadly plague; by then, 24,000 Israelites had already died.

According to Deuteronomy 33, The Israelites are about to enter the Promised Land, Canaan. Moses pronounced blesses on the tribes of Israel before his death. Moses says to the tribes of Zebulun and Issachar the following words:

**May the people of Zebulun prosper in their travels.
May the people of Issachar prosper
at home in their tents.**

**They summon the people to the mountain
to offer proper sacrifices there.
They benefit from the riches of the sea and
the hidden treasures in the sand.**
Deuteronomy 33:18 – 19 NLT

Once the Israelites begin to enter the Promised Land, the Tribe of Zebulun failed to drive out the Canaanites living in the town of Kitron and Nahalol. The Canaanites dwelt among the Tribe of Zebulun and became tributaries, Judges 1:30. The boundaries of Zebulun's land went as far as Sarid. Zebulun's territory was located within Galilee between the Mediterranean and the Sea of Galilee. Zebulun was bordered by the tribes of Issachar, Asher, and Naphtali.

According to the Book of Judges, the Tribe of Zebulun participated in the battle led by Barak and Deborah against Sisera, Judges 4. The Tribe of Zebulun aided Gideon against the army of the Midianites, Judges 6. According to Judges 12:11, the Tribe of Zebulun provided Israel a judge named Elon, and he judged the Israelites for 10 years.

According to 1st and 2nd Chronicles, 50,000 armed men from the Tribe of Zebulun followed David to Hebron to make him king, 1 Chronicles 12. The Tribe of Zebulun joins with Hezekiah in renewing the Passover, 2 Chronicles 30. When King Hezekiah started to amend for the abominations of his father Ahaz, he encouraged the Israelites to keep the Passover. King Hezekiah met resentment, ridicule, and hostility from the people. The Tribe of Zebulun came to Jerusalem, and they destroyed idols, cast all the altars of incense into the brook of Kidron. The Tribe of Zebulun, along with others, kept the fast of the unleavened bread for 7 days with great gladness, 2 Chronicles 30.

Note of Interests: The prophet Isaiah prophesied that in the past God humbled the land of Zebulun and Naphtali, but there will be a time in the future when Galilee of the Gentiles, will be honor and filled with glory, Isaiah 9:1. Isaiah's prediction is Messianic. Galilee including, Zebulun, were the 1st to hear Christ's preaching.

Around 732 BC, the Assyrians conquered the territory of Zebulun, the tribe was exiled, and much of their history was lost.

CHAPTER 18

RIVER KISHON

The Kishon River was approximately 43 miles long in ancient Israel. The Kishon water source originates from Mount Tabor and Mount Gilboa, then flows westward through the Valley of Jezreel, and empty into the Haifa Bay in the Mediterranean Sea, near Mount Carmel.

Note of Interests: The plain of Esdraelon was also called the Valley of Jezreel. It was lowland in northern Israel, which separates the mountain ranges of Carmel and Samaria in the south from those in the areas of Galilee in the north. Haifa Bay is the 3rd largest city in Israel; it stretches along the mountain ridge and foothills of Mount Carmel. Jerusalem and Tel Aviv are the largest cities in Israel.

<hr />

The word "Kishon" is a Hebrew word, which is pronounced "kee-shone," and it means "winding." The word "Kishon" is mentioned only in the Old Testament, a total of 5 times in Joshua 21:28, Judges 4:7, Judges 4:13, Judges 5:21, and 1 Kings 18:40.

Note of Interests: Even though the Kishon River isn't specifically named in the New Testament, scholars believe Jesus Christ would have been very familiar with it. Jesus lived in Nazareth, approximately 13 miles north of the Kishon River.

------◆◆◆◆◆◆------

The Kishon River is the place with two great exceptional incidents occurred in the Israelites history. The Kishon River is relatively modest in size during much of the year. However, during the winter rains, it can become a swollen river, just as it did in ancient times, against Sisera's army.

The Kishon River is mentioned in the Old Testament involving victories of Israel under Barak and Deborah against the Canaanites, and Elijah over the prophets of Baal.

Scholar believes, the part of the Kishon River where the prophets of Baal were slaughtered by Elijah was probably near the spot of Mount Carmel where the sacrifice had taken place. Elijah and the prophets of Baal biblical event must have occurred during the drier season since the Kishon River is referred to as a "brook," unlike in other verses, it is referred to as a "river" or "torrent."

And Elijah said unto them,
Take the prophets of Baal; let not one of them escape.
And they took them:
and Elijah brought them down to the
brook Kishon and slew them there.
1 Kings 18:40 KJV

In Judges 4, Sisera and the Canaanite army were encamped at the Kishon River. The judge and prophetess of Israel named Deborah predicts their defeat. In Judges 5, in

Deborah's song of celebration, the Kishon River is praised for washing away the Canaanite army, which consisted of 900 chariots of iron.

The river of Kishon swept them away,
that ancient river, the river Kishon.
O my soul, thou hast trodden down strength.
Judges 5:21 KJV

PS: If you desire to know more about Rivers, Brooks, Streams, and Water Bodies read <u>Isaiah 26:3 – 4, "Perfect Peace XII" River</u> by Vanessa Rayner.

CHAPTER 19

I WILL DELIVER HIM

The words "I will deliver him" in that exact order is mentioned 4 times in the KJV Bible. The words "I will deliver him" are recorded in 3 verses in the Old Testament, and in one verse in the New Testament. In the Old Testament, the words "I will deliver him" are the words of the LORD in all three verses spoken by Moses, and Deborah. In the New Testament, the words, "I will deliver him" are spoken by Judas Iscariot.

The Book of Deuteronomy is the 1st place where the words "I will deliver him" are mentioned. Deuteronomy begins with Moses speaking to Israel concerning the wilderness journey, and conquest. The Israelites had defeated Sihon, king of the Amorites, Deuteronomy 2:24 – 37.

Deuteronomy 3 speaks on the conquest of Bashan, which was the region east of the Sea of Galilee. The defeat of Og, the king of Bashan, is described in verses 1 – 11 of Deuteronomy 3. When King Og came out to fight Israel at the battle at Edrei, the LORD told Moses don't be afraid because Og will be delivered into Israel's hands.

And the LORD said unto me,
Fear him not:
for I will deliver him, and all his people,
and his land, into thy hand;
and thou shalt do unto him as thou didst
unto Sihon king of the Amorites,

which dwelt at Heshbon.
Deuteronomy 3:2 KJV

Moses recounts the taken of over 60 cities of Bashan with high walls and gated entrance to the people of Israel. The land of the Amorites and Bashan were then given to the tribes of Reuben, Gad, and the half-tribe of Manasseh. The territory was once called the "land of the giants" because Og was from the race of giants.

Note of Interests: Og's framework for his bed was 13½ feet long and 6 feet wide.

As the children of Israel prepare to cross the other side of Jordan River to take the land of Canaan and Jerusalem, Moses commands Joshua to be strong and remember how they defeated Og and Sihon, Deuteronomy 3:21 – 22.

**Ye shall not fear them: for the LORD
your God, he shall fight for you.**
Deuteronomy 3:22 KJV

The 2nd place the words "I will deliver him," is recorded in Judges 4. When Ehud died, the children of Israel again did evil in the sight of the LORD. So, the LORD sold them into the hand of Jabin king of Canaan, who oppressed Israel for 20 years. Jabin was mighty and had 900 chariots of irons. Israel cried out to the LORD.

During this time, Deborah was the judge of Israel. She sent for Barak, and when he arrived, she asked him, "Hath not the LORD God of Israel commanded him to go and draw toward Mount Tabor, and take with him 10,000 men from the tribe of Naphtali and Zebulun?"

Note of Interests: The tribes of Naphtali and Zebulun was closes to Barak than the other tribes.

According to Judge 4:7, Deborah told Barak what the LORD said:

> **And I will draw unto thee to the river Kishon,**
> **Sisera, the captain of Jabin's army, which**
> **his chariots and his multitude;**
> **and I will deliver him into thine hand.**
> Judge 4:7 KJV

After Deborah delivered the words of the LORD to Barak, he said, "If thou wilt go with me, then I will go: But if thou wilt not go with me, then I will not go," Judges 4:8.

The LORD hadn't spoken directly to Barak; He had spoken to Deborah. Barak believed, if the LORD had spoken to Deborah, she would have faith to go to battle with him. Deborah responded, "I will surely go with thee," Judges 4:9.

The next verse where the words, "I will deliver him," is mentioned in Psalm 91:15.

Psalm 91 is known widely by its 1st verse, "He that dwelleth in the secret place of the Most-High shall abide under the shadow of the Almighty." Psalm 91 is considered a "Psalm of Protection," and known as the Soldier's Psalm.

The Midrash believes that Psalm 91 was composed by Moses on the day he completed the building of the Tabernacle in the desert. Psalm 91 has 16 verses that describe Moses' experience when he enters the Tabernacle, covered and surrounded by the Divine Cloud. The next to the last verse of Psalm 91 reads:

> **He shall call upon me, and I will answer him:**
> **I will be with him in trouble; I will**
> **deliver him, and honour him.**
> Psalm 91:15 KJV

The last place the words "I will deliver him," is in the New Testament spoke by Judas, Matthew 26. Jesus' disciples named Judas betrays Him in the Garden of Gethsemane with a kiss, Matthew 26:48.

The 26th chapter of Matthew begins with the passion narrative of Jesus; Matthew 26:1 – Matthew 27:66.

1. The Jewish Leaders Plot to Kill Jesus, Matthew 26:1 – 5
2. The Anointing at Bethany, Matthew 26:6 – 13
3. Judas Agrees to Betray Jesus, Matthew 26:14 – 16

> **Then one of the twelve called Judas Iscariot,**
> **went unto the chief priests, and said unto them,**
> **What will ye give me, and I will deliver him unto you?**
> **And they covenanted with him for thirty pieces of silver.**
> Matthew 26:14 – 15 KJV

4. Jesus Celebrates the Passover with His Disciples, Matthew 26:17 – 25
5. Jesus Institutes the LORD's Supper, Matthew 26:26 – 30
6. Jesus Predicts Peter's Denial, Matthew 26:31 – 35
7. The Prayer in the Garden of Gethsemane, Matthew 26:36 – 46
8. Betrayal and Arrest in Gethsemane, Matthew 26:47 – 56
9. Jesus Faces the Sanhedrin, Matthew 26:57 – 68
10. Peter Denies Jesus, and Weeps Bitterly, Matthew 26:69 – 75

CHAPTER 20
I WILL NOT GO

The words "I will not go" is spoken 9 times in the KJV Bible. They are only spoken in the Old Testament and are listed below. The 1ˢᵗ place the words "I will not go" is mentioned in Exodus 21:5, regarding the law concerning servants who didn't want to leave their masters, after serving them for 6 years.

In the Book of Judges, chapter 4 is where Barak's familiar words, "I will not go," is embedded. Others who spoke the words, "I will not go," were Moses speaking on the law concerning servants and the land of milk and honey, Hobab stating he's returning to his own land, Hannah concerning the child Samuel, a man of God from Judah, Nehemiah regarding fleeing to the temple to save his life, and the words the LORD gave Ezekiel to deliver to the Israelites about their upcoming punishment for their sins.

The 9 verses with the words "I will not go" are as follow.

But if the servant shall plainly say, I love my master, my wife, and my children; <u>I will not go</u> out free: then his master shall bring him unto God, and shall bring him to the door, or unto the doorpost; and his master shall bore his ear through with an awl; and he shall serve him for ever. Exodus 21:5 – 6 ASV

And I will send an angel before thee, that I may cast out the Chanaanite, and the Amorrhite, and the Hethite, and the Pherezite, and the Hevite, and the Jesbusite. That thou mayst enter into the land that floweth with milk and honey. For I will not go up with thee, because thou art a stiffnecked people: lest I destroy thee in the way. Exodus 33:2 – 3 DRA

And Moses said to Hobab, the son of Reuel the Midianite, Moses' father-in-law, We are journeying to the place of which Jehovah said, I will give it unto you: come with us, and we will do thee good; for Jehovah has spoken good concerning Israel. And he said to him, I will not go; but to mine own land, and to my kindred will I go.

Numbers 10:29 – 30 Darby

You shall remember that you were a slave in the land of Egypt, and Yahweh your God redeemed you. Therefore, I command you this thing today. It shall be, if he tells you, "I will not go out from you," because he loves you and your house, because he is well with you, then you shall take an awl, and thrust it through his ear to the door, and he shall be your servant forever. Also, to your female servant, you shall do likewise. Deuteronomy 15:16 – 17 WEB

And Barak said unto her, If thou wilt go with me, then I will go: but if thou wilt not go with me, then I will not go. Judges 4:8 KJV

But Hannah went not up; for she said unto her husband, I will not go up until the child be weaned, and then I will bring him, that he may appear before the LORD, and there abide for ever. 1 Samuel 1:22 KJV

And the man of God said unto the king, "If thou wilt give me half thy house, <u>I will not go</u> in with thee, neither will I eat bread nor drink water in this place; for so was it charged me by the word of Jehovah, saying Thou shalt eat no bread, nor drink water, neither return by the way that thou camest. 1 Kings 13:8 – 9 ASV

I went to the house of Shemaiah the son of Delaiah the son of Mehetabel, who was shut in at his home; and he said, "Let us meet together in God's house, within the temple, and let's shut the doors of the temple; for they will come to kill you. Yes, in the night they will come to kill you." I said, "Should a man like me flee? Who is there that, being such as I, would go into the temple to save his life? <u>I will not go in</u>." Nehemiah 6:10 – 11 WEB

I the LORD have spoken it: it shall come to pass, and I will do it; <u>I will not go</u> back, neither will I spare, neither will I repent; according to thy ways, and according to they doings, shall they judge thee, saith the LORD God. Ezekiel 24:14 KJV

CHAPTER 21
I WILL SURELY GO

The Old Testament and the New Testament have a total of 39 verses with the phrase "I will go." The words "I will go" are mentioned 36 times in the Old Testament, and 3 times in the New Testament. However, the words "I will surely go" are only mentioned twice in the Old Testament.

One dictionary state that "surely" is an adverb, and the word is used to emphasize the speaker's firm belief about what they are saying is true. The word "surely" express that you are certain, without question, undoubtedly, and without fail. A few synonyms for the word "surely" are certainly, undoubtedly, undeniably, of course, with assurance, confidence.

The word "surely" was 1ˢᵗ spoken by the LORD God in the Garden of Eden, Genesis 2.

And the LORD God commanded the man, saying,
Of every tree of the garden thou mayest freely eat:
But of the tree of the knowledge of good
and evil, thou shalt not eat of it:
for in the day that thou eatest thereof
thou shalt surely die.
Genesis 2:16 – 17 KJV

Note of Interests: According to Genesis 2:15 – 17, the LORD God took the man He had created and placed him in the Garden of Eden in to work it and keep it. The LORD

God commanded man that he may eat freely from every tree in the garden except "the tree of the knowledge of good and evil," Genesis 2:17. When reading verses 18 – 24 of Genesis 2, the woman wasn't created yet until verse 22.

And the rib,
which the LORD God had taken from man,
made he a woman,
and brought her unto the man.
Genesis 2:22 KJV

David and Deborah are the two individual that spoke, "I will surely go." David and his troops were preparing to go to battle against David's son, Absalom, and Deborah was preparing to go to battle with Barak against the Canaanites, 2 Samuel 18, and Judges 4.

According to 2 Samuel 18, David mustered the men who were with him. He appointed generals and captains to lead them. David sent the troops out in three groups. One group of troops was under the hand of Joab, another group of troops was under Abishai, and the third group of troops was under the command of Ittai the Gittite. And King David said unto the troops; I will surely go forth with you also, 2 Samuel 18:2.

However, David's troops were against him going to battle with them. In the forest of Ephraim, Absalom's troops were defeated by David's troops. During the battle, Absalom tried to escape on his mule, but his hair got caught in a tree. The mule kept going and left Absalom dangling from the tree. Joab, one of the commanders of King David's army, took 3 daggers and plunged them into Absalom's heart.

However, in the battle with Barak and Sisera, Barak wanted Deborah to go to battle with him. Deborah said, I will surely go with thee: notwithstanding the journey that thou takest shall not be for thine honour; for the LORD shall sell Sisera into the hand of a woman. And Deborah arose and went with Barak to Kedesh, Judges 4:9.

CHAPTER 22

THE LORD SHALL

The words "the LORD shall" are mentioned 188 times, recorded in 182 verses in the KJV Bible; it is mentioned 180 times in the Old Testament, and 8 times in the New Testament. The words "the LORD shall" are mentioned the most in Isaiah, a total of 39 times. The next two books of the Bible in which the words "the LORD shall" are mentioned the most are Deuteronomy (35), and Psalms (24). The Book of Genesis mentions the words "the LORD shall," first, and only one time.

And she called his name Joseph;
and said,
The LORD shall all to me another son.
Genesis 30:24 KJV

The word "shall" express a strong assertion. It makes an idea, impression, or feeling known, and convey what is inevitable likely to happen in the future. The word "shall' is a "modal verb," which expresses necessity or possibility. Other modal verbs are must, will, should, would, can, may, and might. Another dictionary describes "shall" as an "auxiliary verb," which generally appear together with the main verb, to help express the perfect point or thought.

The words "the LORD shall" are mentioned in 29 out of 66 books of the Bible, and a few are listed below.

According to the Book of Exodus, the LORD shall:

1. sever between the cattle Israel and the cattle of Egypt, Exodus 9:4
2. bring thee into the land of the Canaanites, Hittites, Amorites, Hivites, Jebusite, Exodus 13:5
3. fight for you, Exodus 14:14
4. reign for ever and ever, Exodus 15:18
5. give you in the evening flesh to eat, Exodus 16:8

According to the Book of Leviticus, the LORD shall:

1. appear unto you, Leviticus 9:6

According to the Book of Numbers, the LORD shall:

1. do unto us, the same will we do unto thee, Numbers 10:32
2. speak unto me, Numbers 22:8
3. forgive her, Numbers 30:5

According to the Book of Deuteronomy, the LORD shall:

1. scatter you among the nations, Deuteronomy 4:27
2. greatly bless thee in the land, Deuteronomy 15:4
3. command the blessing upon thee, Deuteronomy 28:8
4. establish thee, Deuteronomy 28:9
5. make thee plenteous in goods, Deuteronomy 28:11
6. make thee the head, Deuteronomy 28:13
7. send upon thee cursing, Deuteronomy 28:20
8. cause thee to be smitten, Deuteronomy 28:25
9. bring a nation against thee from far, Deuteronomy 28:49
10. blot out his name from under heaven, Deuteronomy 29:20
11. judge his people, Deuteronomy 32:36

According to the Book of Joshua, the LORD shall:
1.   trouble thee this day, Joshua 7:26

According to the Book of Judges, the LORD shall:
1.   sell Sisera into thine hand, Judges 4:9
2.   rule over you, Judges 8:23

According to the Book of Ruth, the LORD shall:
1.   give thee of this young woman, Ruth 4:12

According to the Book of 1 Samuel, the LORD shall:
1.   have dealt well with my lord, 1 Samuel 25:31

According to the Book of 2 Samuel, the LORD shall:
1.   reward the doer of evil, 2 Samuel 3:39

According to the Book of 1 Kings, the LORD shall:
1.   return his blood upon his own head, 1 Kings 2:32

According to the Book of 2 Chronicles, the LORD shall:
1.   deliver it into the hand of the king, 2 Chronicles 18:11

According to the Book of Psalm, the LORD shall:
1.   judge the people, Psalm 7:8
2.   cut off all flattering lips, Psalm 12:3
3.   swallow them up in his wrath, Psalm 21:9
4.   laugh at him, Psalm 37:13
5.   send the rod of thy strength, Psalm 110:2
6.   increase you more and more, Psalm 115:14
7.   preserve thee from all evil, Psalm 121:7
8.   bless thee, Psalm 128:5

According to the Book of Proverbs, the LORD shall:
1. be thy confidence, Proverbs 3:26
2. reward thee, Proverbs 25:22
3. be made fat, Proverbs 28:25
4. be safe, Proverbs 29:25

According to the Book of Isaiah, the LORD shall:
1. hiss for the fly, Isaiah 7:18
2. have no joy in their young men, Isaiah 9:17
3. rest upon him, Isaiah 11:2
4. utterly destroy the tongue of the Egyptian sea, Isaiah 11:15
5. give thee rest from thy sorrow, Isaiah 14:3
6. smite Egypt, Isaiah 19:22
7. cause his glorious voice to be heard, Isaiah 30:30
8. stretch out his hand, Isaiah 31:3
9. renew their strength; Isaiah 40:31
10. answer; thou shalt cry, ad he shall say, Here I am, Isaiah 58:9
11. guide thee continually, Isaiah 58:11
12. lift up a standard against him, Isaiah 59:19
13. be thine everlasting light, Isaiah 60:20

According to the Book of Jeremiah, the LORD shall:
1. devour from the one end of the land even to the other end, Jeremiah 12:12
2. roar from on high, Jeremiah 25:30
3. answer you, Jeremiah 42:4

According to the Book of Ezekiel, the LORD shall:
1. eat the most holy things, Ezekiel 42:13
2. be in the midst thereof, Ezekiel 48:10

According to the Book of Hosea, the LORD shall:
1. come up from the wilderness, Hosea 13:15

According to the Book of Joel, the LORD shall:
1. utter his voice before his army, Joel 2:11

According to the Book of Micah, the LORD shall:
1. be established in the top of the mountains, Micah 4:1
2. redeem thee from the hand of thine enemies, Micah 4:10

According to the Book of Zechariah, the LORD shall:
1. yet comfort Zion, Zechariah 1:17
2. be seen over them, Zechariah 9:14

In the New Testament, the words "the LORD shall" are only mentioned in 8 of the 27 books and mentioned only once in each book. They are Acts, Romans, Ephesians, 1 Thessalonians, 2 Thessalonians, 2 Timothy, Hebrews, and James.

Acts 2:21, And it shall come to pass, that whosoever shall call on the name of the LORD shall be saved.

Romans 10:13, For whosoever shall call upon the name of the LORD shall be saved.

Ephesians 6:21, But that ye also may know my affairs, and how I do, Tychicus, a beloved brother and faithful minister in the LORD, shall make know to you all things.

1 Thessalonians 4:15, For this we say unto you by the word of the LORD, that we which are alive and remain unto the

coming of <u>the LORD shall</u> not prevent them which are asleep.

2 Thessalonians 2:8, And then shall that Wicked be revealed, whom <u>the LORD shall</u> consume with the spirit of his mouth, and shall destroy with the brightness of his coming:

2 Timothy 4:18, And <u>the LORD shall</u> deliver me from every evil work and will preserve me unto his heavenly kingdom: to whom be glory for ever and ever. Amen.

Hebrews 10:30, For we know him that hath said, Vengeance belongeth unto me, I will recompense, saith the LORD. And again, <u>The LORD shall</u> judge his people.

James 5:15, And the prayer of faith shall save the sick, and <u>the LORD shall</u> rise him up; and if he has committed sins, they shall be forgiven him.

CHAPTER 23

OF A WOMAN

This unique set of words "of a woman" is written in 16 verses in the Bible; 15 verses in the Old Testament and 1 verse in the New Testament. Leviticus (1), Judges (1), 2 Chronicles (1), Job (3), Psalms (2), Isaiah (1), Jeremiah (6), and Galatians (1) are the books in the Bible, which the words "of a woman" are located.

The first place the words "of a woman" is mentioned is in the Book of Leviticus, only one time.

**Thou shalt not uncover, the nakedness
of a woman and her daughter,
neither shalt thou take her son's daughter,
or her daughter's daughter,
to uncover her nakedness; for they
are her near kinswomen:
it is wickedness.**
Leviticus 18:17 KJV

The above scripture is referring to Moses' law. According to the law, if a man married a widow who had a daughter by a previous husband, he was forbidden to marry her. The husband was not allowed to marry the mother's daughter, even after her death. If the daughter was born out of wedlock, the husband was still forbidden to marry her. Leviticus 18:1 – 30, speak on the unlawful marriages, fleshly lusts, incest, and pagan idolatry.

Note of Interests: Antipas broken the law mentioned above by marrying Herodias, Matthew 14:3 – 4. The Egyptians were known to allow marriage between brothers and sisters, and parents with their children. Moses' laws prohibited incestuous relationships. His laws are still adhered to by Christian nations concerning marriage relationships.

The 2nd place where the words "of a woman" is recorded is Judges 4:9. Those words were part of Deborah's answer to Barak when he requested that she go to battle with him at Kedesh.

> **And she said, I will surely go with thee:**
> **notwithstanding the journey that thou**
> **takest shall not be for thine honour;**
> **for the LORD shall sell Sisera into**
> **the hand <u>of a woman</u>.**
> **And Deborah arose, and went to Barak to Kedesh.**
> Judges 4:9 KJV

The 3rd place where the words "of a woman" is recorded is 2 Chronicles 2:14. According to 2 Chronicles 2, Solomon is preparing to build a Temple for the LORD. Solomon sent King Hiram of Tyre a letter asking him to send him cedar, like he sent his father, David. Solomon also asked for a skilled worker trained to work with gold, silver, bronze, iron, and trained in engraving.

King Hiram answered Solomon's letter. He said, "Blessed be the LORD God of Israel who made heaven and earth, who has given King David a wise son, who has discretion and understanding, who will build a temple for the LORD." King Hiram sent a skilled man named Huram-Abi, and he describes him as the son <u>of a woman</u> of the daughters of Dan, and his father was a man of Tyre.

The Book of Job mentioned "of a woman" 3 times. The words "is born" come before "of a woman" each time, and those verses are listed below.

1. Job 14:1, Man that <u>is born of a woman</u> is of few days and full of trouble.
2. Job 15:14, What is man, that he should be clean? And he which <u>is born of a woman</u>, that he should be righteous?
3. Job 25:4, How then can man be justified with God? Or how can he be clean that <u>is born of a woman</u>?

The words "of a woman" are mentioned twice in Psalms; Psalm 48 and 58. Psalm 48 is composed by the sons of Korah. Scholars believe Psalms 46, 47, and 48 is a trilogy and should be read together. They are prayer, worship, and heartfelt emotion toward the presence of God.

Fear took hold upon them there, and pain, as <u>of a woman</u> in travail.
Psalm 48:6 KJV

Scholars believe Psalm 58 was composed by David. Psalm 58 has 11 verses, and at verse 8 are these words, "as a snail which melteth, let every one of them pass away: like the untimely birth <u>of a woman</u>, that they may not see the sun."

David is praying against ungodly men, which the snail represents. He asked may they dissolve into slime, like a miscarriage of a woman's child that never sees the sun.

The Book of Isaiah is the first of the 5 Major Prophet Books. Isaiah 21 is the oracle concerning fallen Babylon. The prophet Isaiah said in verse 3, "Therefore are my loins filled with pain: pangs have taken hold upon me, as the pangs of a woman that travaileth: I was bowed down at the hearing of it; I was dismayed at the seeing of it.

The prophet Isaiah is saying the vision of the destruction of Babylon was terrible that it overpowers him with sharp, grievous pains as the pain of a child-bearing woman.

The Book of Jeremiah records the words "of a woman" the most, a total of 6 times. The prophet Jeremiah mentioned the pain or travail "of a woman" to describe a matter or circumstance in each verse.

The Book of Jeremiah is the 2nd of the Major Prophet Books. Jeremiah lived and prophesied around 627 BC until 586 BC. The Book of Jeremiah has 52 chapters, which stresses disobedience brings judgment, focus on Israel's rebellion, pronounces the coming judgment for Israel, and other nations.

<u>Jeremiah's Statements Against Israel,
Jerusalem, and Judah, Jeremiah 4 – 6</u>

Jeremiah 4:31, For I have heard a voice as <u>of a woman</u> in travail, and the anguish as of her that bringeth forth her first child, the voice of the daughter of Zion, that bewaileth

herself, that spreadeth her hands, saying, Woe is me now! For my soul is wearied because of murderers.

Jeremiah 6:24, We have heard the fame thereof: our hands wax feeble: anguish hath taken hold of us, and pain, as <u>of a woman</u> in travail.

<u>Jeremiah Pronounces Judgment Concerning the Judah's Royal Line, Jeremiah 22</u>

Jeremiah 22:23, O inhabitant of Lebanon, that makest thy nest in the cedars, how gracious shalt thou be when pangs come upon thee, the pain as <u>of a woman</u> in travail!

<u>Jeremiah Pronounces Judgment on Moab, Jeremiah 48</u>

Jeremiah 48:41, Kerioth is taken, and the strong holds are surprised, and the mighty men's hearts in Moab at that day shall be as the heart <u>of a woman</u> in her pangs.

<u>Jeremiah Pronounces Judgment on Syria, Jeremiah 49:23 – 27</u>

Jeremiah 49:22, Behold, he shall come up and fly as the eagle, and spread his wings over Bozrah: and at that day shall the heart of the mighty men of Edom be as the heart <u>of a woman</u> in her pangs.

Jeremiah Pronounces Judgment on Babylon, Jeremiah 50 - 51

Jeremiah 50:43, The king of Babylon hath heard the report of them, and his hands waxed feeble: anguish took hold of him, and pangs as <u>of a woman</u> in travail.

In the New Testament, the Book of Galatians is the only place the words "of a woman," is mentioned.

But when the fulness of the time was come,
God sent forth his Son,
made <u>of a woman</u>,
made under the law,
to redeem them that were under the law,
that we might receive the adoption of sons.
Galatians 4:4 – 5 KJV

CHAPTER 24

HEBER THE KENITE

According to Genesis 15:18 – 21, the Kenites were people living in, near, or around the land of Canaan during the time of Abraham.

> **So the LORD made a covenant with**
> **Abram that day and said,**
> **"I have given this land to your descendants,**
> **all the way from the border of Egypt**
> **to the great Euphrates River,**
> **the land now occupied by the Kenites, Kenizzites,**
> **Kadmonites, Hittites, Perizzites, Rephaites,**
> **Amorites, Canaanites, Girgashites, and Jebusites."**
> Genesis 15:18 – 21 NLT

The Kenites are mentioned in the Book of Genesis (1), Numbers (1), Judges (1), 1 Samuel (3), and 1 Chronicles (1); a total of 8 times in 7 verses in the Bible. In 1 Samuel 15:6 is where the Kenites are mentioned twice in one verse.

According to Exodus 2, Moses killed an Egyptian, hides the body, and later fled from Egypt. Moses fled to Midian, where he met Jethro's 7 daughters, who were shepherdesses. Moses eventually married Jethro's daughter named Zipporah and lived among the Kenites for many years until God called him to deliver the Israelites from the hand of the Egyptians, Exodus 2, and 3.

Moses' father-in-law named Jethro was the priest of Midian. He was also known as Raguel, and a Kenite. Jethro lived south of Canaan near Mount Sinai, and Mount Horeb, Exodus 3:1. The name "Raguel" means "friend of God."

Note of Interests: Scholars believe that the Kenites and Midianites were related. In Numbers 10:29, Moses' father-in-law is called "Raguel the Midianite," elsewhere, he is called a Kenite. In some Bible translations, the name "Raguel" is spelled "Reuel." According to 1 Chronicles 2:55, Kenites are connected to the tribe of the Rechabites. Some scholars believe that the Kenites were descendants of Cain. Other scholars point out that all of Cain's descendants were wiped out during the Biblical Flood, and the Bible makes no connection between the Kenites and Cain.

After Moses delivered the Israelites out of the hand of the Egyptians, Raguel joined Moses and Aaron in bringing a burnt sacrifice and other offerings before the LORD to worship Him, Exodus 18:9 – 12.

The Kenites were friendly to Moses and the Israelites during the time of the exodus. Jethro, Hobab, and other Kenites joined with Moses and traveled to Canaan with the people of God, Exodus 18:1 – 7.

The Kenites settled near Jericho until they eventually moved south to live in the desert region of Negev, Judges 1:16. However, a Kenite named Heber stayed in Canaan, migrating north to near Kedesh. It was Heber's wife named

Jael, who killed Sisera during the time of Deborah and Barak, Judges 4:17 – 23.

During King Saul's reign, the LORD instructed the Israelites to destroy the Amalekites. Saul showed mercy to the Kenites, who lived among the Amalekites because they had shown kindness to the Israelites when they came out of Egypt. Saul told them to move away from the Amalekites, and the Kenites moved away from the Amalekites, 1 Samuel 15.

And Saul said unto the Kenites,
Go, depart, get you down from among the Amalekites,
lest I destroy you with them:
for ye shewed kindness to all the children of Israel,
when they came up out of Egypt.
So the Kenites departed from among the Amalekites.
1 Samuel 15:6 KJV

The Kenites were coppersmiths and metalworkers, much more advanced than the Israelites in this area. The Kenites played a vital role in the history of ancient Israel.

Heber the Kenite was the husband of Jael, and Rechab, the ancestor of the Rechabites, are two others familiar Kenites in the Bible. The wife of Heber the Kenite, named Jael killed Sisera in Judge 4. Then in Judges 5, Deborah mentions Jael, the wife of Heber the Kenite in her song concerning Israel's victory over Sisera and his army.

The Rechabites are the descendants of Rechab through Jehonadab, who accompanied the Israelites into Canaan and dwelt among them. The majority of the Kenites dwelt in cities, but Jehonadab forbade his descendants to drink wine or live in cities.

The name "Heber the Kenite" is mentioned 4 times in 3 verses in the KJV Bible. Heber the Kenite is only mentioned in the Old Testament in the Book of Judges, they are listed below.

Judges 4:11 KJV

Now Heber the Kenite, which was of the children of Hobab the father in law of Moses, had severed himself from the Kenites, and pitched his tent unto the plain of Zaanaim, which is by Kedesh.

Judges 4:17 KJV

Howbeith Sisera fled away on his feet to the tent Jael the wife of Heber the Kenite: for there was peace between Jabin the king of Hazor and the house of Heber the Kenite.

Judges 5:24 KJV

Blessed above women shall Jael the wife of Heber the Kenite be, blessed shall she be above women in the tent.

CHAPTER 25

HOBAB

The name "Hobab" means "beloved" in Hebrew. The word "beloved" means a person that is close to someone's heart, a treasured individual, or someone who is highly regarded. Hobab was an experience sheik of the desert. Hobab's counsel and companionship in the desert were desired by Moses, who was journeying into an unfamiliar region.

Hobab's name is mentioned twice in the Bible, and only in the Old Testament. Both times Hobab's name is mentioned in context with Moses, recorded in Numbers 10:29, and Judges 4:11.

According to Numbers 10:29, Hobab is identified as the son of Raguel the Midianite, Moses' father-in-law. Hobab would be viewed as Moses' brother-in-law. Moses had married his sister named Zipporah, the daughter of

the Midianite priest, Jethro, also known as Raguel. Moses and Zipporah had two sons named Gershom and Eliezer.

Moses tells his brother-in-law, Hobab, that they are journeying to a place which the LORD has said, he will give him.

**And Moses said unto Hobab,
the son of Raguel the Midianite, Moses' father in law,
We are journeying unto the place of which
the LORD said, I will give it you:**

come thou with us, and we will do thee good:
for the LORD hath spoken good concerning Israel.

Numbers 10:29 KJV

Hobab's name is mentioned for the 2nd time in Judges 4, in connection with Moses. In this verse, Hobab is referred to as the father-in-law of Moses.

**Now Heber the Kenite,
which was of the children of Hobab
the father-in-law of Moses,
had severed himself from the Kenites,
and pitched his tent unto the plain of
Zaanaim, which is by Kedesh.**

Judges 4:11 KJV

Note of Interests: Numbers 10:29 describes Hobab as the son of Raguel the Midianite, then there is a comma indicating that the verse is describing Raguel as Moses' father-in-law. Therefore, Hobab is Moses' brother-in-law. However, Judges 4:11 says that Hobab is the father-in-law of Moses. Some scholars believe "Hobab" was another name for Moses' father-in-law "Jethro" like the name "Raguel." This idea coincided with the fact that Jacob was named Israel, and both names are used interchangeably. There are scholars, who believe that Raguel was the father of the clan, and Jethro's daughters were therefore, attributed to Raguel, such as Jacob claiming Joseph's sons as his own in Genesis 48:5. Therefore, this belief would place "Hobab" as Moses' father-in-law, instead of brother-in-law. The problem with this particular idea is that the Bible records Hobab staying with the Israelites as a guide after the exodus from Egypt, Numbers 10:29 – 33; while Jethro is recorded as returning home, Exodus 18:27. Other scholars believe that "Raguel" was Jethro's real name, and "Jethro" was his priestly title because "Jethro" means "excellence." Some hold firm that Hobab was Moses' brother-in-law. Hobab is recorded as being very beneficial during this time to Moses.

CHAPTER 26

THE PLAIN OF ZAANAIM

The KJV Bible has 66 books. There are 39 books in the Old Testament and 27 in the New Testament. However, "the plain of Zaanaim" is only mentioned once in the Old Testament. The name "Zaanaim" in Hebrew means "wanderings." The word "Zaanaim" is also spelled Zaanannim, and Bezaanaim depending on the Bible Translation.

Now Heber the Kenite had separated himself from the Kenites, even from the children of Hobab, Moses' brother-in-law, and had pitched his tent as far as the oak in Zaanannim, which is by Kedesh.
Judges 4:11 WEB

The plain of Zaanaim is mentioned surrounding a great biblical battle between the Canaanites and Israelites. The plain of Zaanaium is where the Canaanites' army under the leadership of Sisera was defeated by Israel's leaders, Barak and Deborah.

Note of Interests: A large area of land, which is normally flat with few trees, and no hills, valleys, or mountains, is considered a plain. According to Joshua 19:33, the plain of Zaanaim was the southern border of the tribe of Naphtali.

The plain of Zaanaim is also where Heber the Kenite pitched his tent. Sisera and his army were losing the battle; he fled on foot about 6 miles from the scene of his defeated army. Sisera then took refuge in Heber the Kenite's tent with his wife. Jael gave Sisera some milk and covered him with a blanket. Sisera then told her to stand at the tent opening, and if anyone comes, and ask her if there is anyone here, to say, no. Sisera fell asleep.

Jael slew Sisera. She drove a tent peg in Sisera's temple as he laid asleep from weariness. Jael went out to meet Barak to have him see what she had done to the man he was seeking.

So on that day Israel saw God defeat
Jabin, the Canaanite king.
Judges 4:23 KJV

The Bible speaks of other plains, where important biblical events took place, also. They are listed below.

1. The plain of Moreh is where Abram passed through when the LORD told him to leave his country, family, and relatives to go to a land He would show him, Genesis 12:1 – 7.
2. The plain of Jordan is the area of land Lot chose, when he separated from Abram, Genesis 13:1 – 12.
3. The plain of Mamre, which is in Hebron, is where Abram dwelt, Genesis 13:18, Genesis 14:13.
4. The plain of the valley of Jericho is the land the LORD showed Moses. The land the LORD promised Abraham, Isaac, and Jacob, Deuteronomy 34:2 – 3.

5. The plain of Medeba unto Dibon was land east of the Jordan River, which Moses gave to the tribes of Reuben, Gad, and half of Manasseh, Joshua 13:8 – 10.

6. The plain of the pillar that was in Shechem is where the leaders of Shechem, the priests, and the military officers met to crown Abimelech king, Judges 9:6

7. The plain of Meonenim is where Abimelech army came out of hiding, and Gaal saw them coming by way of the plain of Meonenim, Judges 9:37

8. The plain of the vineyards is how far Jephthah smote the children of Ammon, Judges 11:32 – 33.

9. The plain of Tabor is where Samuel traveled after anointing Saul king, 1 Samuel 10:3.

10. The plain of the wilderness is where David camped when he fled from Jerusalem after his son Absalom rose against him, 2 Samuel 15:13 – 28.

11. The plain of Jordan is where Huram made bronze furnishing for the Temple into clay molds and had them set up near the plain of Jordan River, between Succoth and Zeredah, 1 Kings 7:46, 2 Chronicles 4:17.

12. The plain of Ono is where Sanballat, Tobiah, Geshem asked Nehemiah to meet them. Nehemiah knew they were planning to harm him, so he sent messengers to them, saying he couldn't stop rebuilding the wall because the work was too important, Nehemiah 6:1 – 4.

13. The plain of Dura, near the city of Babylon, is where King Nebuchadnezzar had a gold statue built that was 90 feet high and 9 feet wide, Daniel 3:1.

14. The plain of Aven is where the LORD said, He would cut off the inhabitant from the plain of Aven, and remove the one who sits on the throne, Amos 1:2 – 5.

CHAPTER 27

THIS IS THE DAY

The phrase "this is the day" is mentioned in the Old Testament only. The phrase is mentioned 5 times in 5 different books of the Bible. The 1st place, "this is the day" is mentioned is in Judges 4. The Book of Judges is the 7th book of the Old Testament, and it belongs to a specific historical tradition called the "Deuteronomic History" along with Deuteronomy, Joshua, 1 and 2 Samuel and 1 and 2 Kings written during the Babylonian Exile.

Deborah, the Judge, and Prophetess of Israel tell Barak, "it's time to attack Sisera and his army! The LORD has already gone ahead of you to fight, and today, Sisera will be defeated by you."

> **And Deborah said unto Barak,**
> **Up; for this is the day**
> **in which the LORD hath delivered**
> **Sisera into thine hand:**
> **is not the LORD gone out before thee?**
> **So, Barak went down from mount Tabor and ten**
> **thousand men after him.** Judges 4:14 KJV

Psalm 118 is the next place the words "this is the day" is recorded in verse 24. The Book of Psalms is divided into 5 books to reflect the 5 books of Moses, which are Genesis, Exodus, Leviticus, Numbers, and Deuteronomy. Psalm 118 is in book 5, which consist of praises to God, and hymns of thanksgiving.

**This is the day which the LORD hath made;
we will rejoice and be glad in it.**
Psalm 118:24 KJV

Note of Interests: Psalm 118 begins and ends with, "O give thanks unto the LORD; for he is good: because his mercy endureth for ever." Also, Psalm 118 has 29 verses, and the words "the LORD" is mentioned in 23 of the 29 verses.

⸻❖⸻

Jeremiah 46:10 is the 3rd verse, "this is the day" is mentioned. The Book of Jeremiah is the 24th book of the Old Testament, but the 2nd book of the Major Prophet Books.

Question: Which books are considered the Major Prophet Books?

Smile
Answer in the back of the book.

1. _____
2. Jeremiah
3. _____
4. _____
5. _____

The Book of Jeremiah is full of prophecies. The phrase "this is the day" is embedded in the prophecy against Egypt and its defeat at Carchemish, Jeremiah 46.

**For this is the day of the LORD God
of hosts, a day of vengeance,
that he may avenge him of his adversaries:
and the sword shall devour,
and it shall be satiate and made drunk with their blood:
for the LORD God of hosts hath a
sacrifice in the north country
by the river Euphrates.**
Jeremiah 46:10 KJV

Lamentations 2:16 is the 4th place; the words "this is the day" is recorded. The Book of Lamentations is the 25th book of the Old Testament, composed of songs of sorrow concerning Jerusalem siege by the Babylonians. Lamentations 2 has 22 verses, which speaks on the LORD's anger at Jerusalem's sin, and He allows their enemies to destroyed them. The enemies have been waiting for this day.

**All thine enemies have opened their mouth against thee:
they hiss and gnash the teeth: they say,
We have swallowed her up:
certainly this is the day that we looked for; we have
found, we have seen it.** Lamentations 2:16 KJV

Ezekiel 39 is the 5th and the last book, in which the words "this is the day" is recorded. The Book of Ezekiel is the 26th book of the Old Testament, and 1 of the Major Prophet Books. The LORD tells Ezekiel to prophesy to Gog, the ruler of the countries Meshech and Tubal. The LORD said, He is Gog enemy, and they are going to be destroyed, die in the mountains, and their flesh will be eaten by birds and animals, Ezekiel 39:1 – 10.

Behold, it is come, and it is done, saith the LORD God; this is the day whereof I have spoken.
Ezekiel 39:8 KJV

CHAPTER 28

THE LORD

The KJV Bible has 31,102 verses. The exact words "the LORD" is mentioned in 5,907 verses in the KJV Bible, while "LORD" is mentioned in 6,667 verses. When "the" is placed in front of a word, it distinguishes or recognizes someone or something. When "the" appears before the word "LORD," it recognizes the Almighty LORD God who rules over all things.

Note of Interests: The word "Lord" in the Bible often refers to the Almighty, the creator of the universe, and the savior of mankind. Jesus is called "Lord" more than "God" in the Bible. Lord refers to someone who rules over others, while God is referred to as a deity, the supreme being, the originator and ruler of the universe. In the religious realm, the Lord and God are used interchangeably.

The word "Lord" can be used as a noun, verb, exclamation, or title. In the Bible, the word "Lord" is printed in all capital letters in many verses, and in some verses the word "Lord" is printed in all lower-case letters. There are also verses in which the letter "L" is capital, while the "ord" letters are in lower-case letters.

The word "Lord" with all capital letters gives thoughts to the original name "YHWH." The biblical reason for the use of the word "LORD" in place of God's Hebrew name

"YHWH" is to respect and follow the traditions of the Israelites. The Israelites did not pronounce or spell out God's name. Therefore, when God's Hebrew name "YHWH" is used in the Old Testament, the translators would use the word "LORD."

The word "Lord" means to have power, authority, or influence over someone or something. The word "Lord" can also refer to a title, and another dictionary records "Lord" as a name for God or Christ.

The words "the LORD" is mentioned the most in the books of Jeremiah (592), Psalms (467), and Deuteronomy (432). Esther, Ecclesiastes, and Song of Songs are the three books in the Old Testament in which the words "the LORD" is not mentioned.

Note of Interests: In the American Standard Version (ASV) Bible, the word "Jehovah" is used rather than "LORD."

--------◆◆◆◆◆--------

The 1ˢᵗ verse in the Bible, where the words "the LORD" is recorded, is Genesis 2:4. God had given the account of creation, Genesis 1 – 2:3, then afterward, He made the following statement:

These are the generations of the
heavens and of the earth
when they were created,
in the day that the LORD God made
the earth and the heavens.
Genesis 2:4 KJV

In the New Testament, the words "the LORD" is mentioned the most in the books of Acts (83), Luke (58), and 1 Corinthians (43). In the New Testament in the books of 1 John and 2 John, the words "the LORD" is not mentioned.

The 1st verse in the New Testament, where the words "the LORD" is mentioned, is Matthew 1:20. In the Gospel of Matthew, Joseph discovered that Mary is pregnant and had considered leaving her, but the angel of the LORD comes to him in a dream and assures him that which is conceived in Mary is of the Holy Ghost.

> **But while he thought on these things,**
> **behold, the angel of the LORD**
> **appeared unto him in a dream,**
> **saying, Joseph, thou son of David,**
> **fear not to take unto thee Mary thy wife:**
> **for that which is conceived in her is of the Holy Ghost.**
> Matthew 1:20 KJV

And the last verse in the Bible, where the words "the LORD" is recorded is in the last chapter of Revelation. Revelation 22 is stating that the prophecy given by the Angel of the LORD to John is true and will take place.

> **And he said unto me,**
> **These sayings are faithful and true:**
> **and the LORD God of the holy**
> **prophets sent his angel to shew**
> **unto his servants the things which must shortly be done.**
> Revelation 22:6 KJV

CHAPTER 29

THE LORD DISCOMFITED

The words "the LORD discomfited" are mentioned twice in the KJV Bible. The KJV Bible has 1,189 chapters; there are 929 chapters in the Old Testament, and 260 chapters in the New Testament.

The words "the LORD discomfited" are only recorded in the Old Testament. The Old Testament has 23,145 verses in 929 chapters, while the New Testament has 7,957 verses in 260 chapters. Out of the 31,102 verses in the entire Bible, "the LORD discomfited" are only recorded in Joshua 10:10, and Judges 4:15.

The word "discomfited" has several meanings. The archaic meaning of "discomfited" is to defeat completely, to vanquish. The word "discomfited" is widely used to mean, to embarrass, confuse, or disconcert. Another meaning of the word "discomfited" that is rarely used is to crush the hopes of a person, making a person feel on edge. The word "discomfited" in the books of Joshua and Judges are referring to their enemy's defeat in battle.

Note of Interests: When the word "LORD" is in all capital letters, it is translating the Hebrew word for the name of God, which is YHWH, or Yahweh. It expresses God in His fullness, Lord and Creator. When the first letter of the word "Lord" is only capitalized, it is because it's the first word of a sentence, or it is referring to 1 of the 3 divine persons of the

Godhead; Trinity. When the word "lord" is in all lower-case letters, it is referring to a human ruler or leader.

The LORD discomfited is mentioned first in the Book of Joshua. According to Joshua 10, the city of Gibeon, along with 3 other towns were being attacked by the 5 kings of the Amorites; Adoni-Zedek the king of Jerusalem, Hoham the king of Hebron, Piram the king of Jarmuth, Japhia the king of Lachish, and Debir the king of Eglon. They all gathered and encamped before the city Gibeon, preparing for war against them.

Joshua and all the mighty men of valor ascended from Gilgal to Gibeon, which is about 15 miles away. The LORD told Joshua to fear not, for He will deliver them into his hand. The LORD defeated the enemies whom Joshua attacked by sending hailstones that fell only on the Amorites, and not the Israelites. The Amorites were thrown into terror, confusion, and defeated at Gibeon.

Joshua 10:10 reads, **"And the LORD discomfited them before Israel, and slew them with a great slaughter at Gibeon, and chased them along the way that goeth up to Bethoron, and smote them to Azekah, and unto Makkedah."**

Note of Interests: According to Joshua 10:14, "And there was no day like that before it or after it, that the LORD hearkened unto the voice of a man: for the LORD fought for Israel."

The next biblical event in which the LORD discomfited is in the Book of Judges. According to Judges 4, when Ehud died, Israel turns away from God again. Israel was conquered by Jabin, the king of Canaan. When Israel cried unto the LORD, he raised up a judge named Deborah, who was also a prophetess.

Deborah summons Barak, an Israelite general, and tells him that God commands him to take 10,000 men from the tribes of Naphtali and Zebulun and attack Sisera, the commander of King Jabin's army. Deborah assures Barak that God will give them victory, but Barak says he'll only go to battle if she goes with him, and she does. Deborah let Barak know that it won't be him who kills Sisera, the captain of Jabin's army, but a woman. Barak leads his 10,000 men against Sisera's army, who had 900 chariots of iron, but they are all killed, except Sisera.

Judges 4:15 reads, **"And the LORD discomfited Sisera, and all his chariots, and all his host, with the edge of the sword before Barak; so that Sisera lighted down off his chariot and fled away on his feet."**

Afterward, Sisera manages to escape to Heber's tent in the plain of Zaanaim. Heber's wife, Jael, goes out to meet Sisera, and tell him, "don't be afraid," Judges 4:18. Sisera tells Jael not to tell anyone he is in the tent and falls asleep. While Sisera is sleeping, Jael takes a tent peg and hammer and drove it into Sisera's temple while he slept, fastening him to the ground, and he died, Judges 4:21.

CHAPTER 30

THE EDGE OF THE SWORD

The phrase "the edge of the sword" is mentioned 37 times in 34 verses in the KJV Bible. In the verses of Deuteronomy 13:15, Joshua 8:24, and 1 Samuel 22:10, the phrase "the edge of the sword" is mentioned twice. The Old Testament records "the edge of the sword" in 32 verses, while the New Testament only mentions it in Luke 21:24, and Hebrew 11:34.

The sword in biblical times was a very deadly weapon since both edges cut with equal effectiveness. The sword was used with forcibly strikes, swings, and swipes in any direction. A dagger-like sword with a double-edged blade was used for stabbing when fighting at close range.

The phrase "the edge of the sword" is mentioned the most in the books of Joshua and Judges. The edge of the sword is mentioned in 12 verses in the Book of Joshua, and 8 verses in Judges. The Book of Joshua records Joshua's leadership, conquered of the land of Canaan, and how it was divided among the Israelites. The Book of Judges recounts Israel's conquest of the land of Canaan under the leadership of the 12 judges.

Note of Interests: In the book of Joshua and Judges, the Israelites had just entered the Promised Land, Canaan.

They were in constant warfare with the inhabitants of the territory, and the Lord kept giving them the victory.

The phrase "the edge of the sword" is mentioned twice in the books of Deuteronomy, 1 Samuel, and Job. In the books of Genesis, Exodus, Numbers, 2 Samuel, 2 Kings, Jeremiah, Luke, and Hebrews, "the edge of the sword" is mentioned once.

The 34 verses are listed below that contain the phrase "the edge of the sword" with a brief title. I pray you take time to read each chapter that contains the phrase "the edge of the sword;" Be Bless in Jesus' Name.

Dinah and the Shechemites, Genesis 34:1 – 31

And they slew Hamor and Shechem his son with the edge of the sword, and took Dinah out of Shechem's house, and went out, Genesis 34:26.

Israel Defeats the Amalekites, Exodus 17:8 – 16

And Joshua discomfited Amalek and his people with the edge of the sword, Exodus 17:13.

Israel's Victory over Sihon and Og, Numbers 21:21 – 35

And Israel smote him with the edge of the sword, and possessed his land from Arnon unto Jabbok, even unto the children of Ammon: for the border of the children of Ammon was strong, Numbers 21:24.

A Warning Against Idolatry, Deuteronomy 13:1 – 18

Thou shalt surely smite the inhabitants of that city with the edge of the sword, destroying it utterly, and all this is therein, and the cattle thereof, with the edge of the sword, Deuteronomy 13:15.

Instructions for Destroying the Nearby Cities, Deuteronomy 20:1 – 20

And when the LORD thy God hath delivered it into thine hands, thou shalt smite every male thereof with the edge of the sword, Deuteronomy 20:13.

The Jericho Defeated by Joshua and the Israelites, Joshua 6:1 – 27

And they utterly destroyed all that was in the city, both man and woman, young and old, and ox, and sheep, and ass, with the edge of the sword, Joshua 6:21.

The Israelites Defeat Ai, Joshua 8:1 – 29

And it came to pass, when Israel had made an end of slaying all the inhabitants of Ai in the field, in the wilderness wherein they chased them, and when they were all fallen on the edge of the sword, until they were consumed, that all the Israelites returned unto Ai. And smote it with the edge of the sword, Joshua 8:24.

Israel Destroys the Southern Towns; Makkedah 1st, Joshua 10:28 – 43

And that day Joshua took Makkedah, and smote it with the edge of the sword, and the king thereof he utterly destroyed, them, and all the souls that were therein; he let none remain: and he did to the king of Makkedah as he did unto the king of Jericho, Joshua 10:28.

Israel Attacks Libnah, Joshua 10:29 – 30

And the LORD delivered it also, and the king thereof, into the hand of Israel; and he smote it with the edge of the sword, and all the souls that were therein; he let none remain in it; but did unto the king thereof as he did unto the king of Jericho, Joshua 10:30.

Joshua and the Israelites Attacked Lachish, Joshua 10:31 – 33

And the LORD delivered Lachish into the hand of Israel, which took it on the 2nd day, and smote it with the edge of the sword, and all the souls that were therein, according to all that he had done to Libnah, Joshua 10:32.

Joshua and the Israelite Army went on to Eglon, Joshua 10:34 – 35

And they took it on that day, and smote it with the edge of the sword, and all the souls that were therein he utterly destroyed that day, according to all that he had done to Lachish, Joshua 10:35.

Israel Left Eglon and Attacked Hebron, Joshua 10:36 – 37

And they took it, and smote it with the edge of the sword, and the king thereof, and all the cities thereof, and all the souls that were therein; he left none remaining, according to all that he had done to Eglon; but destroyed it utterly, and all the souls that were therein, Joshua 10:37.

Joshua and the Israelites Attacked Debir, Joshua 10:38 – 43

And he took it, and the king thereof, and all the cities thereof; and they smote them with the edge of the sword, and utterly destroyed all the souls that were therein; he left none remaining: as he had done to Hebron, so he did to Debir, and to the king thereof; as the had done also to Libnah, and to her king, Joshua 10:39.

Israel Defeats the Northern Armies of Canaan, Joshua 11:1 – 23

And they smote all the souls that were therein with the edge of the sword, utterly destroying them: there was not any left to breathe: and he burnt Hazor with fire, Joshua 11:11.

Joshua Captured Hazor and Killed Its King

And all the cities of those kings, and all the kings of them, did Joshua take, and smote them with the edge of the sword, and he utterly destroyed them, as Moses the servant of the LORD commanded, Joshua 11:12.

The Israelites took All the Plunder

And all the spoil of these cities, and the cattle, the children of Israel took for a prey unto themselves; but every man they smote with the edge of the sword, until they had destroyed them, neither left they any to breathe, Joshua 11:14.

The Land Given to Dan, Joshua 19:40 - 48

And the coast of the children of Dan went out too little for them: therefore the children of Dan went up to fight against Leshem, and took it, and smote it with the edge of the sword, and possessed it, and dwelt therein, and called Leshem, Dan, after the name of Dan their father, Joshua 19:47.

The Tribe of Judah Attacked and Captured Jerusalem, Judges 1:1 – 18

Now the children of Judah had fought against Jerusalem, and had taken it, and smitten it with the edge of the sword, and set the city on fire, Judges 1:8.

The Descendants of Joseph Attacked the Town of Bethel, Judges 1:22 – 26

And when he shewed them the entrance into the city, they smote the city with the edge of the sword; but they let go the man and all his family, Judges 1:25.

Deborah said, the LORD has given Sisera into your Hands, Judges 4:4 – 15

And the LORD discomfited Sisera, and all his chariots, and all his host, with the edge of the sword before Barak; so that Sisera lighted down off his chariot and fled away on his feet, Judges 4:15.

Barak Chased, Judges 4:16 – 24

But Barak pursued after the chariots, and after the host, unto Harosheth of the Gentiles: and all the host of Sisera fell upon the edge of the sword; and there was not a man left, Judges 4:16.

The Tribe of Dan Attacked Laish, Change its Name to Dan, Judges 18:27 – 31

And they took the things which Micah had made, and the priest which he had, and came unto Laish, unto the people that were at quiet and secure: and they smote the with the edge of the sword and burnt the city with fire, Judges 18:27.

Israel Fights with the Tribe of Benjamin, Judges 20:1 – 48

And the liers in wait hasted and rushed upon Gibeah; and the liers in wait drew themselves along and smote all the city with the edge of the sword, Judges 20:37.

And the men of Israel turned again upon the children of Benjamin, and smote them with the edge of the sword, as well the men of every city, as the beast, and all that came to hand: also they set on fire all the cities that they came to, Judges 20:48.

Israel Help Provide Wives for the Tribe of Benjamin, Judges 21:1 – 25

And the congregation sent thither twelve thousand men of the valiantest, and commanded them, saying, God and smite the inhabitants of Jabeshgilead with the edge of the sword, with the women and the children, Judges 21:10.

King Saul Defeats the Amalekites, 1 Samuel 15:1 – 9

And he took Agag the king of the Amalekites alive, and utterly destroyed all the people with the edge of the sword, 1 Samuel 15:8.

King Saul had 85 Priests and their Family Slaughter, 1 Samuel 22:11 – 23

And Nob, the city of the priests, smote he with the edge of the sword, both men and women, children and sucklings, and oxen, and asses, and sheep with the edge of the sword, 1 Samuel 22:19.

Absalom Rebel Against His Father, King David, 2 Samuel 15:1 – 37

And David said unto all his servants that were with him at Jerusalem, Arise, and let us flee; for we shall not else escape from Absalom: make speed to depart, lest he overtake us suddenly, and bring evil upon us, and site the city with the edge of the sword, 2 Samuel 15:14.

Jehu Kills the Priests and Worshipers of Baal, 2 Kings 10:18 – 31

And it came to pass, as soon as he had made an end of offering the burnt offering, that Jehu said to the guard and to the captains, Go in, and slay them; let none come forth. And they smote them with the edge of the sword; and the guard and the captains cast them out and went to the city of the house of Baal, 2 Kings 10:25.

Job's 1ˢᵗ Test, Job 1:6 – 22

And the Sabeans fell upon them, and took them away; yea, they have slain the servants with the edge of the sword; and I only am escaped alone to tell thee, Job 1:16.

While he was yet speaking, there came also another, and said, The Chaldeans made out three bands, and fell upon the camels, and have carried them away, yea, and slain the servants with the edge of the sword; and I only am escaped alone to tell thee, Job 1:17.

Jeremiah's Message to King Zedekiah, Jeremiah 21:1 – 10

And afterward, saith the LORD, I will deliver Zedekiah king of Judah, and his servants, and the people, and such as are left in this city from the pestilence, from the sword, and from the famine, into the hand of Nebuchadnezzar king of Babylon, and into the hand of their enemies, and into the hand of those that seek their life: and he shall smite them with the edge of the sword; he shall not spare them, neither have pity, nor have mercy, Jeremiah 21:7.

<u>Jesus Speaks About the Future</u>, Luke 21:5 – 38

And they shall fall by the edge of the sword and shall be led away captive into all nations: and Jerusalem shall be trodden down of the Gentiles, until the times of the Gentiles be fulfilled, Luke 21:24.

<u>People of Faith</u>, Hebrews 11:1 – 40

Quenched the violence of fire, escaped the edge of the sword, out of weakness were made strong, waxed valiant in the fight, turned to flight the armies of the aliens, Hebrews 11:34.

CHAPTER 31

NOT A MAN LEFT

The phrase "not a man left" is mentioned in the KJV Bible 3 times, and only in the Old Testament. The phrase "not a man left" is mentioned first in Joshua 8. The 8th chapter of Joshua has 35 verses and can be outlined as follow.

1. The Lord's Plans to Defeat the Town of Ai, Joshua 8:1 – 13
2. Israel Successfully Destroys the Town of Ai, Joshua 8:14 – 23
3. The King of Ai, Hung on a Tree, Joshua 8: 24 – 29
4. Joshua Reads the Blessings and Curses, Joshua 8:30 – 35

Joshua 8:17 reads, **"And there was not a man left in Ai or Bethel, that went not out after Israel: and they left the city open, pursued after Israel."** This verse is surrounding the Israelites destroying the town of Ai.

God encouraged Joshua and gave him instructions on how to defeat Ai. God told Joshua do not be afraid nor dismayed and take all the people to war with him. Joshua and the Israelites put all the inhabitants of Ai to the sword, burned their city, hung their king, and then Joshua gave all the plunder to the soldiers. After the battle victory, Joshua built an altar unto the LORD God of Israel about 20 miles from Ai.

123

The next time the phrase "not a man left" is mentioned in the Book of Judges, chapter 4. The 4th chapter of Judges has 24 verses and can be outlined as follow.

1. Deborah, Israel 4th Judge, Judges 4:1 – 5
2. Deborah Summoned Barak, Judges 4:6 – 11
3. Sisera Summoned His 900 Chariots of Irons, Judges 4:12 – 16
4. Sisera Fled on Foot to the Tent of Jael, Judges 4:17 – 20
5. Heber's Wife, Jael, Kills Sisera, Judges 4:21 – 24

Judges 4:16 reads, **"But Barak pursued after the chariots, and after the host, unto Harosheth of the Gentiles: and all the host of Sisera fell upon the edge of the sword; and there was not a man left."** This verse is surrounding Deborah and Barak's victory.

According to Judges 4, the children of Israel, the Israelites did evil in the sight of the LORD again. They fell back into idolatry, and the LORD sold them into the hand of Jabin king of Canaan as Israel punishment. After 20 years of oppression, the children of Israel cried unto the LORD.

By Divine instructions, Deborah ordered Barak to raise an army, and engage in war with Jabin's forces. Barak insisted that she go to war with him, and she did. Sisera was the commander of Jabin's forces. He had 900 chariots of irons, but Israel didn't. In the end, God gave Deborah and Barak the victory. Sisera's army was defeated, every soldier was put to death by the sword, and a woman named Jael killed Sisera.

The 3rd time the words "not a man left" is mentioned in 2 Kings, chapter 10. The 10th chapter of 2 Kings has 36 verses and can be outlined as follow.

1. Jehu Writes the Leaders of Samaria, 2 Kings 10:1 – 5
2. Leaders of Samaria Kill Ahab's Children, 2 Kings 10:6 – 11
3. Jehu Kills Ahaziah's Relatives, 2 Kings 10:12 – 14
4. Jehu Meets Jehonadab, 2 Kings 10:15 – 17
5. Jehu Destroyed the Worshippers of Baal, 2 Kings 10:18 – 29
6. Jehu's Rule Over Israel, 2 Kings 10:30 – 31
7. Hazael, King of Aram Defeats Israel, 2 Kings 10:32 – 33
8. The Death of Jehu, 2 Kings 10: 34 – 36

2 Kings 10:21 reads, **"And Jehu sent through all Israel: and all the worshippers of Baal came, so that there was not a man left that came not. And they came into the house of Baal; and the house of Baal was full from one end to another."** This verse is surrounding Jehu and how he killed Ahab's Baal worshippers, and the entire family line of Ahab.

Jehu was the 10th king of the northern Kingdom of Israel. He executes the house of Ahab at Jezreel, and then slew all Ahab's descendants in Samaria. Jehu uses deception to get all the prophets of Baal, his servants, and priests to come to the temple to hold a great sacrifice for Baal. All of Baal's worshippers came for this great occasion, not a man that worshipped Baal stayed at home. Jehu then ordered the guards to kill everyone in the temple.

Jehu was raised to power by God to destroy Baal worship in Israel and to exterminate King Ahab's family line. Jehu fulfilled Elijah's prophecy, he gave to Ahab and Jezebel following the scandal of Naboth's vineyard, and his death caused by Ahab and Jezebel, 1 Kings 21. Elijah had prophesied to King Ahab and Jezebel that God was going to eliminate his family.

A READER'S QUESTION

This new section just dropped in my spirit at 0613 on January 14, 2017, titled <u>A Reader's Question</u>.

I had a brief conversation with a lady at Bible Study. In the conversation, she said, she enjoyed the Bible Study, I spoke well and wished she wasn't afraid to speak in front of people.

Even though this isn't a question, I gave her a response/answer, similar to this: I used to stutter really bad, when I tried to talk, and that made me very shy. I still don't pronounce some words clearly.

When God called me to be a MAP, I fasted and cried out to Him for 40 days and 40 nights. Father God removed a great deal of my shyness and gave me enough courage to pray, teach, and preach His word in front of people when needed.

There are still times the enemy reminds me of my speech issues and attempts to bring fear upon me; so that I will stutter. I had to decide deep down in my soul if no one understands what I'm saying, I know God does, and that is all that matters to me.

The key to overcoming your fear of speaking in front of people is fasting, along with praying and seeking God, even the more. Hallelujah!

**In all thy ways acknowledge him,
and he shall direct thy paths.**
Proverbs 3:6 KJV

AUTHOR'S CLOSING REMARKS

May God Bless You! I must say, "writing this book was a delight." I enjoyed the way each chapter in this book reinforces the subtitle of this book; <u>Judges 4:1 – 16</u>. Even though the subtitle states verse 1 – 16 is what the following chapters would be about, all 24 verses of Judges 4 where touched on, in one way, or another.

I was thrilled how each chapter blended with some of the other chapters but in a slightly different fashion. I will be able to cleave to this particular biblical event surrounding Deborah and Barak because the facts and details overlap each other. I hope and pray you will, too. Glory be to God!

Oh Heavenly Father . . .

I wouldn't mind doing another book, like this one. But nevertheless, not my will but your will. Amen

Pray for the Ministry . . . *May the "Prince of Peace," give you "His Peace."*

Dr. Vanessa

REFERENCES

Chapter 1
1. BibleGateway: https://www.biblegateway.com
2. Wikipedia, The Free Encyclopedia: https://en.wikipedia.org/wiki/Book_of_Judges

Chapter 2
3. BibleGateway: https://www.biblegateway.com

Chapter 3
1. BibleGateway: https://www.biblegateway.com
2. Wikipedia, The Free Encyclopedia: https://en.wikipedia.org/wiki/Bees

Chapter 4
1. BibleGateway: https://www.biblegateway.com
2. Jacksonville Theology Seminary: The Children of Israel

Chapter 5
1. BibleGateway: https://www.biblegateway.com
2. Wikipedia, The Free Encyclopedia: https://en.wikipedia.org/wiki/Ehud

Chapter 6
1. BibleGateway: https://www.biblegateway.com
2. Jacksonville Theology Seminary: The Historical Kings

Chapter 7
1. BibleGateway: https://www.biblegateway.com

Chapter 8
1. BibleGateway: https://www.biblegateway.com
2. Wikipedia, The Free Encyclopedia: https://en.wikipedia.org/wiki/Sisera

Chapter 9
1. BibleGateway: https://www.biblegateway.com
2. Wikipedia, The Free Encyclopedia: https://en.wikipedia.org/wiki/Waters_of_Merom

Chapter 10
1. BibleGateway: https://www.biblegateway.com
2. Wikipedia, The Free Encyclopedia: https://en.wikipedia.org/wiki/Three_Age_System

Chapter 11
1. BibleGateway: https://www.biblegateway.com
2. Wikipedia, The Free Encyclopedia: https://en.wikipedia.org/wiki/Arecaceae

Chapter 12
1. BibleGateway: https://www.biblegateway.com
2. Jacksonville Theology Seminary: Bible's Cities, Towns, and Villages

Chapter 13
1. BibleGateway: https://www.biblegateway.com
2. Wikipedia, The Free Encyclopedia: https://en.wikipedia.org/wiki/Barak

Chapter 14
1. BibleGateway: https://www.biblegateway.com

Chapter 15
1. BibleGateway: https://www.biblegateway.com
2. Wikipedia, The Free Encyclopedia: https://en.wikipedia.org/wiki/Mount_Tabor

Chapter 16
1. BibleGateway: https://www.biblegateway.com
2. Wikipedia, The Free Encyclopedia: https://en.wikipedia.org/wiki/Naphtali

Chapter 17
1. BibleGateway: https://www.biblegateway.com
2. Wikipedia, The Free Encyclopedia: https://en.wikipedia.org/wiki/Tribe_of_Zebulun

Chapter 18
1. BibleGateway: https://www.biblegateway.com
2. Wikipedia, The Free Encyclopedia: https://en.wikipedia.org/wiki/Kishon_River

Chapter 19
1. BibleGateway: https://www.biblegateway.com
2. Wikipedia, The Free Encyclopedia: https://en.wikipedia.org/wiki/Psalm_91
3. Wikipedia, The Free Encyclopedia: https://en.wikipedia.org/wiki/Matthew_26

Chapter 20
1. BibleGateway: https://www.biblegateway.com

Chapter 21
1. BibleGateway: https://www.biblegateway.com
2. Merriam-Webster: https://www.merriam-webster.com/thesaurus/surely

Chapter 22
1. BibleGateway: https://www.biblegateway.com

Chapter 23
1. BibleGateway: https://www.biblegateway.com
2. Wikipedia, The Free Encyclopedia: https://en.wikipedia.org/wiki/Psalm_48
3. Wikipedia, The Free Encyclopedia: https://en.wikipedia.org/wiki/Psalm_58

Chapter 24
1. BibleGateway: https://www.biblegateway.com
2. Wikipedia, The Free Encyclopedia: https://en.wikipedia.org/wiki/Kenites

Chapter 25
1. BibleGateway: https://www.biblegateway.com
2. BibleGateway Encyclopedia: https://www.biblegateway.com/resources/encyclopedia-of-the-bible/Hobab

Chapter 26
1. BibleGateway: https://www.biblegateway.com
2. BibleGateway Encyclopedia: https://www.biblegateway.com/wiki/Zaanaim

Chapter 27
1. BibleGateway: https://www.biblegateway.com

Chapter 28
1. BibleGateway: https://www.biblegateway.com

Chapter 29
1. BibleGateway: https://www.biblegateway.com
2. Wiktionary, The Free Dictionary: https://en.wiktionary.org/wiki/discomfit

Chapter 30
1. BibleGateway: https://www.biblegateway.com

Chapter 31
1. BibleGateway: https://www.biblegateway.com
2. Jacksonville Theology Seminary: Joshua
3. Jacksonville Theology Seminary: Deborah and Barak
4. Jacksonville Theology Seminary: The Historical Kings

ANSWERS & INFORMATION SECTION

Chapter 1

What is the 7th book in the New Testament?

1st Corinthians written by Paul

Chapter 3

Who was Isaac's parents?

Isaac's birthplace was Canaan, Israel, and his parents were Abraham and Sarah. Isaac had two sons, who were twins, named Jacob and Esau.

Chapter 15

Which disciples were with Jesus during his transfiguration?

According to Mark 9:2, After six days, Jesus took Peter, James, and John with him and led them up a high mountain, where they were all alone. There he (Jesus) was transfigured before them.

Chapter 27

The Major Prophet Books are Isaiah, Jeremiah, Lamentations, Ezekiel, and Daniel.

Printed in the United States
By Bookmasters